Racial Unity
An Imperative for Social Progress

Racial Unity

An Imperative for Social Progress

Richard W. Thomas

Published by the Association for Bahá'í Studies

Special Conference Edition

Bahá'í Studies Publications, Ottawa, Canada

© 1990 by the Association for Bahá'í Studies
All rights reserved, including the right of
reproduction in part or in whole in any form
without the written permission of the Publisher,
The Association for Bahá'í Studies, 34 Copernicus
Street, Ottawa, Ontario, Canada, K1N 7K4.

Printed in Canada on recycled paper

ISBN 0-920904-23-8

To my black and my white students
may they come to understand
how the power of racial unity
can transform the world

Contents

Foreword ix

Part One: Why Racial Unity is an Imperative for Social Progress in the Modern World

Chapter 1:   Racial Unity: An Imperative for Social Progress
in America and other Multiracial Societies.................   1

Chapter 2:   European Global Conquest and Expansion and
the Emergence of the Ideology of White Racial
Superiority in America...   11

Chapter 3:   Thomas Jefferson's View of Multiracial America........   19

Part Two: Barriers to Racial Unity and Multiracial Progress

Chapter 4:   White Manifest Destiny and the Victimization
of Native and African Peoples....................................   35

Chapter 5:   The Legacy of White Racism in the Twentieth
Century..   61

Part Three: The Interracial Struggle for Racial Justice, Unity, and Fellowship

Chapter 6:   The Other Tradition in American Race Relations........   83

Chapter 7:   Towards a Model of Racial Unity: Bahá'í
Teachings and Community Practices...........................   95

Epilogue

Chapter 8:   A Transformational Agenda for Racial
Unity and Social Progress...   121

Foreword

This book has been germinating for many years. As a teacher and researcher in both African-American history and race relations, I have been discussing many of these issues in my courses with my students for close to twenty years. My initial interest in race relations originated from several sources: the primary source is the Bahá'í community in the United States, which has provided me with a human laboratory where I have been able to experience first-hand the interaction among racially and culturally diverse peoples. For nearly thirty years I have not only observed a process of community building among these diverse peoples but also witnessed a transformation of their traditional prejudices, fears, and anxieties into bonds of interracial and multicultural fellowship. I have watched and been involved in the painful process of confronting racism within this community, and I have experienced along with others the joy of working through the various stages of white racism and black bitterness to interracial bonding. This process continues.

The second source of my interest in race relations grew out of my involvement in the Civil Rights Movement as a young black student. Observing blacks and whites marching together confirmed my belief in the imperative of racial unity for the social good of the United States and the world.

The third source of my interest has been the classroom where for over twenty years I have been able to teach students from many racial backgrounds—but mainly blacks and whites—about the history of racism and how best to combat it and to work together for the achievement of a multiracial society based on justice, love, and fellowship. In a way, this book has been written for them.

The title of this book, *Racial Unity: An Imperative for Social Progress,* originated from a series of lectures I gave at various universities in Canada and the United States during the late 1980s. As a result of long years of teaching about the history of racism, I felt compelled to include the history of "the other tradition" of American race relations, namely: the history of the interracial struggle for racial justice, unity, love, and fellowship. People needed to know, I reasoned, both the history of racism *and* the history of those who have struggled against racism and have envisioned a social order in which people not only accept each other as equal but also have a profound appreciation of each other as members of the one human family. So, in one sense, this brief and very general historical essay is a statement of my belief and dearest hope that black and white Americans can transcend their common racial history and create a truly racially just, loving society that can be a model of unity for the world to emulate.

Acknowledgements

This book is the product of many devoted people. Foremost among them is Christine Zerbinis of the editorial board of the Association for Bahá'í Studies who coordinated the work of all those involved in the heroic effort of getting this book ready in time for the Model of Race Unity Conference in Atlanta. Two of my graduate students, Kyungsik Irene Shim and Shobha Ramanand, also deserve a special note of thanks, Shobha for her extensive library work in verifying references and Irene for her long hours spent assisting me in historical research. Her considerable skills proved invaluable in the final stages of checking sources. Several readers contributed their time in reading portions of the manuscript: the main ones included Professor Harry Reed, History Department, Michigan State University, and Professor Ruth Harris, Department of Afro-American Studies Center, State University of New York, Brockport.

Part I

**Why Racial Unity
is an Imperative for Social
Progress in the Modern World**

CHAPTER 1

RACIAL UNITY: AN IMPERATIVE FOR SOCIAL PROGRESS IN AMERICA AND OTHER MULTIRACIAL SOCIETIES

> Among the moral imperatives of our time, we are challenged to work all over the world with unshakable determination to wipe out the last vestiges of racism. . . .We know full well that racism is still the hound of hell which dogs the tracks of our civilization.
>
> Dr. Martin Luther King, Jr.

Racism has cost the world dearly. Systems of white domination in the Americas, Asia, and Africa have left a trail of blood and anguish down through history that has imposed upon the present generation a legacy of hatred and racial conflict. Centuries of white racial dominance have created centuries of racial distrust among nonwhites—centuries of distrust that have festered into countless manifestations of racial disunity in every multiracial society in the world. We have only to turn our attention to the periodic racial disruptions in the United States, South Africa, and England to see what the future might continue to be like for those multiracial societies that fail to address their racial problems effectively.[1]

Multiracial nations have just begun to realize the global impact of their domestic racism and the extent to which their individual countries can be suddenly sucked into a racial maelstrom of international magnitude. Many citizens of multiracial societies fail to understand the connection between their domestic racial policies and world peace. In 1976, an editorial in the *Detroit Free Press* alerted its readers to such a connection when it warned: ". . .a lot of history is bearing down on us now. . .and the implications of. . .racial conflict, not only throughout Southern Africa, but throughout much of the world, are ominous."[2]

The global ramifications of domestic racism and conflict became clearer as concerned scholars and journalists began writing on the subject, particularly during the era of urban racial turmoil in the United States. In 1967, the year of the Detroit race riot, the worst race riot in American history, Ronald Segal published a book entitled *The Race War* in which he described the future of global

---

1. John Benyon and John Solomos, "British Unrest in the 1980s" 3-22; Stuart Hall, "Urban Unrest in Britain" 45-50, in John Benyon and John Solomos, eds., *The Roots of Urban Unrest* (Oxford: Pergamon Press, 1987); John Rex, "Racialism and the Urban Crisis," *Race, Science and Society* (Paris and London: The UNESCO Press, 1975) 262-300; Jonathan Kaufman, *Broken Alliance: The Turbulent Times between Blacks and Jews in America* (New York: Mentor, 1988); Lena Williams, "Officials Voice Growing Concern over Racial Incidents on U.S. Campuses." *The New York Times*, December 15, 1986, p. 2; "Black Rage, White Fist," *Time,* August 5, 1985.

2. Editorial, *Detroit Free Press*, September 21, 1976.

race relations in the following terms: "In a world where the white rich seek to preserve an order against which the colored poor rebel, the central fact of the past will increasingly be seen as the domination of the one by the other, just as the central fact of the future will increasingly emerge as the struggle between them." Justifying the provocative title of his book, he continued: "The phrase 'race war' is a strong one, but no stronger, I believe, than the steadily increasing hostility between white and nonwhite fully warrants. The two colors are physically clashing in a dozen parts of the world already, whether through riots in the slums of American cities or the engagement of guns in South Vietnam and Angola." Therefore, Segal argued, "It is the contention of this book that the occasions for clash must multiply, and the war grow ever more intense, unless the circumstances which provoke the antagonisms of race are themselves removed."[3]

It was not to be. The "antagonisms of race" remain virtually untouched throughout the potential racial hotspots of the world.[4]

Although some citizens of multiracial societies have just begun to understand that social and economic justice are preconditions for racial unity and that racial unity is an imperative for social progress, some multiracial societies such as the United States and South Africa are still paying the cost for refusing to learn this lesson. What is the reason for this blind and irrational refusal to abandon racial prejudice in these societies? Why have the dominant white groups in America and South Africa clung to their ideologies of white supremacy for so long? What is it about racial superiority that makes it so appealing to some segments of these societies that for example South Africa cannot imagine treating all human beings fairly?

Fortunately, there are great signs of hope operating throughout the world. As bad as apartheid is in South Africa, it has generated an international movement composed of people from many nations, races, and religious backgrounds dedicated to the elimination of apartheid. This international anti-apartheid movement is transforming the face of the planet, bonding many people who previously knew or cared little about their common humanity. In America, where the resurgence of racism has understandably frightened and angered many people who grew up during the Civil Rights Movement believing in "the Beloved Community," where there is still much white resistance to and deliberate-

---

3. Ronald Segal, *The Race War* (New York: Viking Press, 1967) vii-1. This theme of race war has been echoed through the centuries by such observers of race relations as Thomas Jefferson and W.E.B. DuBois; see discussion of Jefferson in Chapter 3 and of DuBois later in this chapter.

4. Throughout the late 1970s and 1980s, blacks in the South African townships, particularly Soweto, rebelled against the system of apartheid. In Britain during the 1980s, racial conflicts erupted in several cities, including Brixton, Handsworth in Birmingham, Sheffield, and Tottenham in London. In America, the worst racial conflicts of the 1980s broke out in May 1980 in Miami, Florida. See, Solomos, 3-14; Harris Joshua and Tina Wallace with the assistance of Heather Booth, *To Ride the Storm: The 1980 Bristol "Riot" and the State* (London: Heineman, 1983) 56-210; "Black Rage, White Fist" 24-28; "Confronting Racial Isolation in Miami" (Washington, D.C.: U.S. Commission on Civil Rights, June 1982, v. 26).

misunderstanding of such policies as affirmative action, and where blacks and whites in most major metropolitan areas are more segregated than ever before, brave bands of multiracial people are struggling against racism and racial conflicts. Groups and organizations such as Mothers against Racism in California, the Interracial Family Alliance, Focus Hope in Detroit, and the race unity programs of the American Bahá'í community are more than just isolated "points of lights." Rather, they represent a new consciousness within many multiracial societies that social progress in multiracial societies is impossible without racial justice and unity. [5]

The United Nations has long recognized the connection between racial justice and unity and the social progress within the global community. One of the United Nations' many organs, the Sub-Commission on Prevention of Discrimination and Protection of Minorities, was set up in 1947 by the Commission on Human Rights. It was given the mandate "to undertake studies, particularly in the light of the Universal Declaration of Human Rights, and to make recommendations to the Commission on Human Rights concerning the prevention of discrimination of any kind. . .and the protection of racial, national, religious and linguistic minorities." In 1949, a group of experts on racial problems, meeting in Paris under the auspices of UNESCO, pointed out that the "biological fact of race and the myth of 'race' should be distinguished." In 1951, UNESCO convened a second meeting of scientists who, among similar conclusions, stated in their Statement on the Nature of Race and Racial Differences, that "available scientific knowledge provides no basis for believing that the groups of mankind differ in their innate capacity for intellectual and emotional development." UNESCO convened several other conferences on race in Moscow in 1964 and again in Paris in 1967. The latter conference focused on race and racial prejudice and adopted the Paris Statement on Race and Racial Prejudice. The final statement points to racism as the main problem: "The human problems arising from so-called 'race' relations are social in origin rather than biological. The basic problem is racism, namely, anti-social beliefs and acts which are based on the fallacy that discriminatory intergroup relations are justifiable on biological grounds." [6]

---

5.   The most dramatic example of this international movement against apartheid was seen in the world tour of Nelson Mandela, the leader of the African National Congress. However, many ordinary people also participated in this global movement for racial justice. For example, in 1984, eleven supermarket employees in Ireland were fired when they refused to handle South African fruit. After three years of pickets at the store, a court decided that the employees had been unfairly dismissed. See: Martin Gottlieb, "Mandela's Visit, New York's Pride," *New York Times*, June 24, 1990, 13; Marcus Eliason, "Irish Eyes Smile upon Mandelas," *Lansing·State Journal*, July 2, 1990; Focus Hope was started in Detroit about a year after the 1967 riot. See, Richard W. Thomas, "Looking Forward: The Detroit Experience after the Riots of 1943 and 1967" in Benyon and Solomos, 150; Mothers for Race Unity and Equality was founded by LeNeice Jackson-Gaertner in the late 1980s, leaflet, "Mothers for Race Unity and Equality," see parts 3 and 4 for information on the Interracial Family Alliance and the Bahá'í Community.

6.   Herman Santa Cruz, *Racial Discrimination* (New York: United Nations, 1971) 13, 22.

From the late 1960s to the present, the United Nations and its organs have played a major role in confronting racism through the global community. In 1983 the General Assembly "proclaimed the ten-year period beginning on 10 December 1983 the Second Decade to Combat Racism and Racial Discrimination." Building on its earlier work in the first Decade to Combat Racism and Racial Discrimination, the General Assembly approved the Program of Action for the Second Decade which included among its activities seminars on combating racism and racial discrimination. International efforts to combat racial discrimination within the global community have drawn attention to the fact that racism is not just limited to such countries as America and South Africa. Racism started as an international social virus, and it remains so today. Its most virulent strains are to be found in South Africa and America, yet the virus is present in every multiracial society in the world. Some multiracial societies such as England and Brazil might have less pathological racial histories, but they share the disease of racism and must treat it effectively or suffer long-term socially debilitating effects·[7]

At the present time many multiracial societies are struggling to find the best solutions to their racial problems. Shaken by racial conflicts and riots over the last few decades, America, England, and South Africa have tried a variety of approaches to ensure "domestic peace" but have ignored the root causes of their racial problems. In the wake of their most recent riots, both America and England initiated various race relations programs, including race-awareness conferences, multiracial/cultural organizations, and a host of scholarly productions on the "racial problem."[8] South Africa still lags far behind these two other multiracial societies.

America and England could serve as models for South Africa, saving it from many more decades of racial turmoil, if they could put their own racial houses in order. They could do this by educating the present generation of their citizens about the urgency of establishing racial justice and unity in their respective societies. Citizens of multiracial societies must be made aware of the relationship between racial unity and social progress. They must be exposed to the great historical cost in human misery and social conflict that racism has exacted from the entire society. They must be made to understand that there cannot be any lasting peace in any multiracial society without genuine love and fellowship

---

7. For more recent information on the United Nations work in the area of elimination of racism and racial discrimination, see: *Seminar on International Assistance and Support to Peoples and Movements Struggling against Colonialism, Racism, Racial Descrimination and Apartheid* (New York United Nations, 1986) 1. While Brazil's racial problems have not reached the volatile stage of racial problems in the United States, England, and South Africa, the country does have "problems" related to race. For example, there has been a tendency among certain groups in Brazil to see themselves as a "racial democracy" and to avoid serious discussion of racial discrimination in the country. See Thomas E. Skidmore, "Race and Class in Brazil: Historical Perspectives" in Pierre-Michel Fontaine, ed., *Race, Class and Power in Brazil* (Los Angeles: Center for Afro-American Studies, University of California, 1985) 11-21.

8. See part 6 in Benyon and Solomos; since Detroit had the worst race riot of the 1960s, its post-riot developments embodied valuable lessons for other cities; see, Thomas, 150-51.

among racial groups. Then, it must be demonstrated to them that such love and fellowship among the various races of their societies will not only reduce and ultimately eliminate racism and racial conflicts but also elevate the entire society to new levels of material and spiritual development.

To accomplish this realization among the citizenry of multiracial societies, we will need a new paradigm to improve understanding of historical and contemporary race relations as related to social progress. People must realize that there is an organic relationship between racial justice and unity and social progress. We must understand that in today's complex, interdependent world in which peoples from diverse racial and cultural backgrounds are increasingly interacting in thousands of new settings, racial unity has become an imperative for social progress. Social and economic progress in every multiracial society today is dependent on the degree to which racial groups learn to live, work, and play together in love and harmony. Where racial unity based upon social justice and nurtured by love and fellowship is lacking or absent, such multiracial societies are forced to waste precious time, energy, and resources managing crises.

The First Universal Race Congress, 1911, London
An Early Effort to Understand the Significance
of Race in the Modern World

As we survey the persistent forms of racism and racial discrimination throughout the world, particularly in South Africa and the United States, we realize that we still have a long way to go in the struggle to eliminate "the last vestiges of racism." Long before the late Martin Luther King, Jr. spoke of this task as the "moral imperative of our age," the great black American scholar W.E.B. DuBois, writing in 1903, placed it on the social agenda of the twentieth century: "The problem of the twentieth century is the problem of the color-line,—the relation of the darker to the lighter races of men in Asia and Africa, in America and the islands of the sea."[9] DuBois wrote these words from his office at Atlanta University where he was then a professor, already on his way to becoming one of America's greatest writers and scholars in the field of race relations. He would spend his entire life struggling against racism in America and abroad. When he died in the early 1960s, disillusioned and bitter in self-exile in Ghana, West Africa, racism, "the hound of hell," was still dogging the tracks of our civilization.

W.E.B. DuBois's deep concern for racial justice for the darker peoples of the world led him and his NAACP co-worker Mary White Ovington to attend the Universal Race Congress held in 1911 in London, England. Franz Boas, the famous anthropologist, and Charles A. Eastman, an American Indian scholar, were among the other Americans who attended this historic interna-

---

9.   W.E.B. Dubois, *The Souls of Black Folk* (Chicago: A.C. McClung and Co., 1904) 13.

tional gathering. According to the organizers, the object of the Congress was "to discuss in the light of science and the modern conscience, the general relations subsisting between the peoples of the West and those of the East, between so-called whites and so-called colored peoples, with a view to encouraging between them a fuller understanding, the most friendly feelings and a heartier co-operation."[10] Thoughtful and concerned men and women around the world had come to the conclusion that something had to be done to address the problems of race. European racial dominance over millions of nonwhite natives could not but lead to racial hatred and conflict. Clearly, the world could not progress with millions of nonwhites oppressed in body and spirit by white governments that placed the social and economic progress of the white race above the rights and dignity of nonwhite races.

The First Universal Race Congress occurred during a decade characterized by what one scholar has described as "the proliferation of international conferences and agencies, and the intensification of movements for national dignity and independence—as revolutions from China to Mexico and the great 'dress rehearsal' in 1905 that shook the Czar's Empire."[11]

Racial developments of various historic import also marked this decade. Uprisings in Africa, notably on the French Ivory Coast and the one racial event that traumatized the white world and forced it to confront both its racial arrogance and its vulnerability—the Japanese defeat of Russia. A little over a decade earlier, blacks from various parts of the African Diaspora had met in London, convening the first Pan African Congress. DuBois attended this Congress as its secretary.[12]

While race was the key concern of the Universal Race Congress, world peace also occupied a central place on the agenda. However, Gustav Spiller, one of the major organizers of the Congress and the spiritual leader of the London Ethical Culture movement and author of several books on education and psychology, and DuBois, then a leading expert on American race relations and social conditions among black Americans, were in the minority of those who linked race to peace.

In his paper "The Problem of Race Equality," Spiller argued that "if the brotherhood of man is to become a reality, as poets and prophets have fondly dreamed, and if the great nations of the world, irrespective of race, are to create a World Tribunal and a World Parliament, it is indispensable that the leading varieties of mankind shall be proved substantially equals."[13] In an unsigned

---

10. G. Spiller, ed., *Inter-Racial Problems: Papers from the First Universal Race Congress Held in London in 1911* (New York: Citadel Press, 1970) 1970 Introduction 6; 1911 Introduction xiii, 99-103, 367-77.

11. G. Spiller, ed., *Inter-Racial Problems*: see Herbert Aptheker's 1970 introduction to this volume, 5.

12. Spiller, 5.

13. G. Spiller, " The Problem of Race Equality," in Spiller, *The Race Congress* 30.

commentary on the Congress published in *The Crisis* during the Fall of 1911, DuBois painted a visionary picture of the potential of the Congress: "When fifty races look each other in the eye, face to face, there arises a new conception of humanity and its problems. . . .On the whole the view of the race problems of the world as revealed in the Congress was strongly reassuring; but of this was clear. It was because the men themselves were there."[14]

The presence of people from all racial backgrounds at the Congress impressed DuBois, but more important was the presence of representatives from many of the oppressed racial groups speaking on behalf of their own people. "In their absence," DuBois pointed out, "a terrible indictment against 'lazy' Negroes, 'dishonest' Chinese, and 'incompetent' Asians could have been framed; but in the face of gentlemen from various human races of all shades and cultures. . ." some white Americans and Europeans found the burden of affirming their racism a bit more difficult.[15]

Obviously pleased with the major thrust of the Congress and the racial climate at the social events where racial unity and fellowship prevailed, DuBois commented, "It seems no exaggeration to say that a few Congresses like this would do more for the unity of mankind and reasonable sympathy between the races, [and] the stop of war, slavery and oppression than any other single movement."[16]

The Bahá'í approach to the problems of race was one of several presented at the Congress. However, the Bahá'í view placed more emphasis on racial unity and harmony. Unable to attend himself, 'Abdu'l-Bahá (1844-1921), the son of Bahá'u'lláh, the prophet-founder of the Bahá'í Faith and the appointed leader of that Faith from 1892-1921, sent a message to the gathering in which he explained the importance and beauty of diversity in the human family. He asked the gathering to consider the varieties of flowers in a garden and how they "seem but to enhance the loveliness of each other," and "when differences of color, ideas, and character are found in the human Kingdom, and come under the control of the power of Unity, they too show their essential beauty and perfection." 'Abdu'l-Bahá explained in his letter that rivalry between "the different races of mankind was [*sic*] first caused by the struggle for existence among the wild animals. This struggle is no longer necessary: nay rather! interdependence and co-operation are seen to produce the highest welfare in nations. The struggle that now continues is caused by prejudice and bigotry."[17] According to 'Abdu'l-Bahá, there was only one way to address such problems:

Today nothing but the power of the Divine Word, which embraces the Reality

---

14. "The Race Congress," *The Crisis*, September, 1911, 207, 209.

15. "The Race Congress" 208.

16. "The Race Congress" 208.

17. Spiller in *The Race Congress* 156.

of all things, can draw together the minds, hearts and spirits of the world under the shadow of the heavenly Tree of Unity. The Light of the Word is now shining on all horizons. Races and nations, with their different creeds, are coming under the influence of the Word of Unity in love and in peace. . . .

The call to arbitration, to peace, to love, and to loyalty is the call of Baha'u'llah. His standard floats since fifty years summoning all of whatever race and creed.[18]

"This Congress is one of the greatest of events," 'Abdu'l-Bahá proclaimed in his letter. "It will be for ever to the glory of England that it was established at her capital. It is easy to accept a truth; but it is difficult to be steadfast in it; for the tests are many and heavy."[19] Realizing how difficult it would be to carry out such a task, to go beyond the reading of scholarly papers and idealistic statements, of which the world had had its fill, 'Abdu'l-Bahá urged the Congress not to become just a "thing of words." "O ye people! cause this thing to be not a thing of words, but of deeds. Some Congresses are held only to increase differences. Let it not be so with you. Let your effort be to find harmony. Let Brotherhood be felt and seen among you; and carry ye its quickening power throughout the world. It is my prayer that the work of the Congress will bear great fruit."[20]

As the key organizer of this historic event, Gustav Spiller must have been optimistic about future Congresses. He drafted and sent to delegates a printed memorandum marked confidential, in which he urged them to see the Congress as the springboard from which could launch a worldwide "Association for the Promotion of Inter-Racial Concord." He encouraged the delegates when they returned home to hold public meetings and to establish local branches of this worldwide Association. Several months later, at least one such meeting was held in New York addressed by Felix Adler and W.E.B. DuBois. But, as historian Herbert Aptheker said so well in his excellent commentary on this noble effort by Spiller, "The realities of economics, of imperial conflicts, and of strategic considerations—on the whole conspicuously absent in the deliberations of the Congress—worked their inexorable way and 1914 marked not the holding of the Second Universal Race Congress, but rather the commencing of World War 1!"[21]

Notwithstanding the tragic interruption of war, the prayers of 'Abdu'l-Bahá and the optimism of W.E.B. DuBois were not in vain. As Aptheker said so well: "Nevertheless the First Universal Congress did represent some of the noblest

---

18. "The Race Congress" 156.

19. "The Race Congress" 157.

20. "The Race Congress" 157.

21. Aptheker, in Spiller, 14.

ideals of Humanity; it did bring together men and women of all climes and all colors; it did project the vital vision of a world comity of Peoples and it did serve as educator and inspirer of thousands seeking a fraternal and creative and peaceful way of life."[22] In 1912 'Abdu'l-Bahá visited North America where he gave many talks on the relationship between racial unity, love, and fellowship.[23] DuBois never forgot this First Universal Race Congress. Fifty years later, he wrote about it in his autobiography: "It was a great and inspiring occasion bringing together representatives of numerous ethic and cultural groups and bringing new and frank conceptions of scientific bases of racial and social relations of people."[24]

The world paid a high price in human misery, racial hatred, and conflict when it failed to assume the challenges put forward by the more thoughtful delegates at the First Universal Race Congress. While race was not the major factor causing the Great War, it contributed to the burden of human suffering surrounding the conflict.

---

22. Aptheker, in Spiller, 14-15.

23. Allen L. Ward, *239 Days: 'Abdu'l-Bahá's Journey in America* (Wilmette, Illinois: Bahá'í Publishing Trust, 1977) 40; 'Abdu'l-Bahá, *The Promulgation of Universal Peace*, 2d ed. (Wilmette, Illinois: Bahá'í Publishing Trust, 1982).

24. W.E.B. Du Bois, *The Autobiography of W.E.B. DuBois* (New York: International Publisher, 1968) 263.

CHAPTER 2

EUROPEAN GLOBAL CONQUEST AND EXPANSION AND THE EMERGENCE OF THE IDEOLOGY OF WHITE RACIAL SUPERIORITY IN AMERICA

> The race to which we belong is the most arrogant and rapacious, the most exclusive and indomitable in history. It is the conquering and unconquerable race, through which alone man has taken possession of the physical and moral world. All other races have been its enemies or its victims.
>
> J. J. Ingalls
> Speech to the United States Senate, 1890

The modern world is still paying the social costs of historic racism. We are only just beginning to understand the extent to which the system of racial domination imposed upon millions of non-Europeans by European nations over the past few centuries still governs the conscious and unconscious relationships between whites and nonwhites throughout the world. Racism has wounded generations of nonwhites far more deeply than whites will ever know. Many whites, however, still partake of the privileges of color bequeathed to them by the legacy of historic racism, unable or unwilling to divest themselves from the advantages of being "white" in a world that still touts white cultural values and allocates rewards for accepting such values. As a result, racial fear and hatred still dominate interracial interactions in most multiracial societies.

Everywhere we look today, in America, England, and South Africa, we observe the long hand of racism reaching across the centuries into the present. The black underclass in American cities, trapped in poverty, crime, and violence, is not composed of disconnected entities floating in time and space. These blacks are the human flotsam and jetsam of a historical process of dehumanization that started with the first slave ship that landed in the English colonies. The angry black students in Soweto, South Africa, who refuse to go to school under an apartheid educational system, are linked by the same history of white racial dominance. Native-American adults and youth seeking escape through drugs and alcohol, as well as the Hispanic and Indo-Chinese struggling to carve a niche for themselves in a world in which whites largely determine the size and shape of the niches, all share a common history of racial victimization that still exerts tremendous influence throughout the global community.

The Role of African Slavery in the Development of Global Racism

The above should be not interpreted as a wholesale indictment of the white race. Rather, it should be viewed as an indictment of a historical system of racial dominance that developed in parallel to the European world economy from the sixteenth century onwards. Almost imperceptibly at first, Europeans developed racist attitudes towards Indians, Africans, and other nonwhites as they went about their business exploring the "New World," conquering the indigenous peoples and then taking their lands, and buying and selling Africans to till these lands. The European banking houses, ship captains, planters, soldiers, and sailors, and a host of other "whites" who participated in this Grand Adventure were not necessarily evil people. Like people of all ages and nations, they found themselves thrust into a historical process that many neither fully understood nor controlled. For example, the unquestioned evils of the African slave trade that drove Western civilization down the long path of racial turmoil, the contemporary by-products of which periodically rise up to greet us on the front pages of our morning newspaper in the form of racial conflicts, began in part as a response to a shortage of labor. As Immanuel Wallerstein has argued:

> But why Africans as. . .the slaves? Because of the exhaustion of the supply of laborers indigenous to the region of the plantations, because Europe need-ed a source of labor from a reasonably well-populated region that was acces-sible and relatively near the region of usage. But it had to be from a region that was outside its world-economy so that Europe could feel unconcerned about the economic consequences for the breeding region of wide-scale removal of manpower as slaves. Western Africa filled the bill best.[1]

Before the fateful choice was made to make West Africans the main labor force for the New World plantation systems, Europeans in their greed for more land and profits had committed genocide and near genocide of the Indian populations. Indian populations on most Caribbean islands "disappeared entirely." In New Spain (Mexico), the Indian population numbered about 11 million in 1519. By 1650, the population had declined to about 1.5 million. Indian populations in Brazil and Peru experienced a similar decline. Some scholars have argued that the two key factors responsible for the decline in indigenous populations were the disease and damage "to Indian cultivation caused by domestic animals that the Europeans bred." But, the most likely explanation for the decline seems to be have been the "sheer exhaustion of manpower, especially in the mines."[2] In short, the Indian populations were practically killed off by varying means,

---

1. Immanuel Wallerstein, *The Modern World-System: Capitalist Agriculture and the Origins of the European World-Economy in the Sixteenth Century* (New York: Academic Press, 1976) 66.

2. Wallerstein, *The Modern World-System* 67.

brought on by the imposition of an European-based world economy reinforced by racial selection.

The early brutal exploitation of Indian and African labor by Europeans set the stage for similar exploitation of nonwhite labor throughout the European world-system. By the late nineteenth century, European nations had carved up Africa and subjugated millions of nonwhites in various parts of Asia.

The European exploration of the "New World" in the fifteenth century led to centuries of brutal conquest, colonization, and protracted wars of extermination. At the same time that the indigenous peoples were being systemically forced from their lands by the use of subterfuge and guns, millions of Africans were being forcibly removed from their homelands by international slave cartels to supply the labor needs of plantations in the New World. Millions of Africans died on their way to the slave ships; others died crossing the ocean; still others died or were maimed and murdered while laboring on plantations established to satisfy the needs of European planters, merchants, and banking houses.

The New World alone could not satiate the appetite of a Europe that had lost its soul in pursuit of material gain. All the lands populated by non-Europeans found themselves the target of European mercantile capitalism. Wherever a European ship could sail and find a sponsor to make a profit, the people and the land and resources upon or beneath it became fair game for the global market, dominated by a people who would soon consider such domination their divine right simply by virtue of race and culture.

The Emergence of the Ideology of White Superiority

As Europeans increasingly took over the lands and/or the resources of non-Europeans in Asia, Africa, the Americas, New Zealand, Australia, and various other regions of the world dominated by Europeans on behalf of "White Christian Civilization," they increasingly saw themselves as the stewards of world civilization, placed on earth to elevate and guide the nonwhite masses. This collective feeling of racial superiority developed gradually over the centuries as the European peoples established contact with non-European peoples for the purposes of conquest and exploitation.[3] The English played a leading role both in the conquest of peoples of color and the development of the ideology of racial superiority.

According to historian Winthrop Jordan, the English had a peculiar disposition toward racist feelings about blacks: "In England perhaps more than in southern Europe, the concept of blackness was loaded with intense meaning. Long before they found that some men were black, Englishmen found in the idea of blackness a way of expressing some of their most ingrained values. No

3. E. Franklin Frazier, *Race and Culture Contacts in the Modern World* (Boston: Beacon Press, 1957) passim.

other color except white conveyed so much emotional impact."[4]

According to *The Oxford English Dictionary*, before the sixteenth century, the meaning of black in English culture had the following connotations: "Deeply stained with dirt; soiled, dirty, foul. . . .Having dark or deadly purposes, malignant; pertaining to or involving death, deadly; baneful, disastrous, sinister. . .iniquitous, atrocious, horrible, wicked. . . .Indicating disgrace, censure, liability to punishment, etc."[5] Jordan continued to explain the deep-seated cultural symbolism of blackness within the collective psyche of the English. "Black was an emotionally partisan color, the handmaid and symbol of baseness and evil, a sign of danger and repulsion." But, if blackness symbolized everything negative in the English collective mind, what about whiteness? "Embedded in the concept of blackness," Jordan explains, "was its direct opposite—whiteness. No other colors so clearly implied opposition. . . ."[6] What preceded the establishment of African slavery in America and the subsequent development of ideological racism as a rationale and defense for the practice was an historical and cultural predisposition among the English populace that saw blackness as embodying everything negative. It is necessary, then, to probe further into the English cultural history to understand what happened to them when they became "white" Americans. Jordan explains further:

> White and black connoted purity and filthiness, virginity and sin, virtue and baseness, beauty and ugliness, beneficence and evil, god and the devil. Whiteness, moreover, carried a special significance for Elizabethan Englishmen: it was, particularly when complemented by red, the color of perfect human beauty, especially female beauty. This ideal was already centuries old in Elizabeth's time, and their fair Queen was its very embodiment: her cheeks were "roses in a bed of lilies."[7]

An adoring nation knew precisely what a beautiful Queen looked like. This "adoring nation" visualized their queen in the following manner:

> Her cheeke, her chinne, red neck, her nose, This was a lillye, that was a rose; Her bosome, sleeke as Paris plaster, Held up two bowles of Alabaster.[8]

The English were no less enthnocentric than other peoples who also saw themselves as the standard of all beauty. Most certainly at this point in their cultural history they were acting quite normally. The ideal for them was just

---

4. Winthrop D. Jordan, *The White Man's Burden: Historical Origins of Racism in the United States* (New York: Oxford University Press, 1974) 5-6.

5. Quoted in Jordan, 6.

6. Jordan, 6.

7. Quoted in Jordan, 6.

8. Jordan, 6.

that: "Her cheeke, her chinne, . . .This was a lillye, that was a rose. . . ." The beauty standards of the English had evolved over the centuries before they made contact with black Africans. The English voyagers were about a century behind Portugal's Prince Henry the Navigator in making contact with Africans. When they did make contact around 1550, the African's color arrested their attention probably more than anything else. In some ways, one could say the English suffered an intense cultural shock due mainly to the trauma of being thrown into sudden contact with people so very different from them in terms of color. Here again, Jordan explains this process: "The powerful impact which the Negro's color made upon Englishmen must have been partly owing to suddenness of contact. Although the Bible as well as the arts and literature of antiquity and the Middle Ages offered some slight introduction to the 'Ethiope', England's immediate acquaintance with black-skinned peoples came with relative rapidity."[9]

The English had known people much darker than themselves, but few as black as the West Africans. To them, northern Africans, whom they referred to as Moors, were really black. In Shakespeare's time, the Moors were considered dark, and the terms *Negro* and *black* carried the same connotations. When the English made contact with the really "black" peoples of West Africa, they began refining their first perceptions. They called these blacks, "black Moors." "The impact of the Negro's color was the more powerful upon Englishmen, moreover, because England's principal contact with Africans came in West Africa and the Congo," Jordan argues "which meant that one of the lightest-skinned of the Earth's peoples suddenly came face to face with one of the darkest."[10]

Where, then, did this English cultural predisposition towards "blackness" place black people? Where did blacks fit in the English standards of beauty? If one had to be lily-white with red cheeks to be beautiful, certainly then, the West Africans were nowhere on the English scale of beauty. "By contrast, the Negro was ugly, by reason of his color and also his 'horrid Curles' and 'disfigured lips and nose'," Jordan states. A century after their first sustained contact with West Africans, the English were still struggling with the social and psychological ramifications of blackness. Their discovery of the black African made their "whiteness" all the more dear. Such contrast in color in such a short period of time proved too much. Whiteness had to be right and correct and divine. Yet, many English writers of the period understood that Africans also had their own standards of beauty based on blackness. Indeed, in 1621, one English writer probably shocked his readers by reporting that some Africans painted the devil white in contempt for the color.[11]

In Great Britain, probably more so than in any other European country, the duality of black and white permeated the literature. There were indeed few European cultures whose literature abounded with such black and white symbolism as England's. William Shakespeare used this symbolism in such plays

9.   Jordan, 5.

10.   Jordan, 5.

11.   Jordan, 6-7.

as *The Merchant of Venice, Titus Andronicus,* and *Othello.* William Blake also made use of such symbolism in his poem, "The Little Black Boy."[12]

Reading about black Africans and interacting with them a safe distance from home provided one kind of unique experience. However, when planters began bringing blacks into Britain, it created problems. As blacks started arriving in Britain in large enough numbers to be noticed, it was not long before voices were being raised against them, led by Queen Elizabeth herself. In 1596, the queen sent a letter to the Lord Mayor of London and other cities, complaining that there were of late too many blacks in the country. By 1601, the queen felt the problem was so severe, particularly because of the poverty of many people during this period, that she issued a royal proclamation ordering all "blackamoors" out of the kingdom. The royal proclamation proved ineffective because by the end of sixteenth century, the black minority had not only become "sufficiently large to cause the government concern," but some blacks had by then also gained their freedom and were participating in the local churches. Others were independent enough to pay their own taxes, and a smaller group even owned property. Twenty years after Queen Elizabeth's efforts to rid Britain of its blacks, this tiny minority had "firmly integrated itself into socially acceptable positions." By early Stuart England, blacks were being employed as servants. By 1660, after the Restoration, blacks were being reinstated "in the ranks from which Elizabeth had tried to dislodge them."[13]

By this time, the historical combination of English involvement in the African slave trade and their cultural predisposition towards blackness had evolved into a set of racist values appropriate for formulating a fairly formidable ideology of racism. Many of these values were brought by those English who later settled America. There was not only a continual transatlantic interchange of commodities and people but also an interchange of dominant values, theories, and practices concerning blacks. In fact, the system of African slavery under the English created one of the most sophisticated forms of white racial dominance and ideological racism. As one scholar explains this development:

> It was in the British plantation colonies in the Western hemisphere that race relations emerged in their clearest form: the whites, as masters, were the superior race; the blacks, as slaves, were the inferior race. A basically similar model of race relations also emerged in the Eastern hemisphere once the British had consolidated their hold over the Indian sub-continent.[14]

America and Britain were well on their way to becoming racist societies

---

12. Lemeul Johnson, *The Devil, the Gargoyle, and the Buffoon: The Negro as Metaphor in Western Literature* (Port Washington, N.Y.: Kennikat Press, 1969) 38, 54.

13. James Walvin, *The Black Presence: A History of the Negro in England* (New York: Schocken Books, 1972) 12-13.

when they became dependent on African slave labor. This dependency would not have necessitated an ideology based upon racism had these societies been able to reconcile their religious, moral, and political traditions with African slavery and the conquest of the native peoples.

Virginia's economic need for plentiful cheap labor drove state legislators to write slavery into law in 1660. Soon other colonies followed this example.[15] The American Revolutionary War and the post-war period presented some problems of how the new nation would resolve the fundamental moral and political contradiction of holding slaves while preaching and fighting for freedom. As it would also successfully do in future situations, America fashioned a special brand of political and moral compromise that helped it to rationalize both the conquest of the native peoples as well as the enslavement of blacks. Since America was not about to abandon slave labor or its policy of dispossessing the native peoples of their land, the only real and practical choice was to minimize the nature of its sins: blacks and the native peoples (Indians) were not to be considered on the same level of humanity as whites; blacks were heathen and amoral, next to the apes in the scale of evolution. Gradually an ideology emerged in America and Britain which explained that white racial dominance was a blessing. "It was not until the slave trade came to require justification," Jordan points out, "that some Englishmen found special reason to lay emphasis on the Negro savagery."[16]

As slavery continued to become more profitable to America and Britain, the moral contradictions became more apparent and blatant. Both countries began formulating a racist ideology to cover those moral contradictions that collided with certain Christian and Enlightenment beliefs in the universality of the human race. By the eighteenth century, there emerged a wide array of antiblack theories and views of which racist apologists could have their choice. There was the work of Dr. Charles White, a famous English physician and surgeon, who developed so-called scientific arguments for the multiple origins of the human race. He believed that blacks occupied a different "station" on the human scale than whites, indeed, that blacks comprised an intermediate species between the whites and the apes.[17] Another scholar, Lord Kames, also contributed his share to the development of the ideology of racism. This Scottish jurist argued that blacks were not even of the same species as whites.[18] Voltaire believed that both Indians and blacks comprised separate species. Thomas Jefferson joined in the parade of dignitaries who believed that nonwhites were

14. Dilip Hiro, *Black British, White British*, rev. ed. (New York and London: Monthly Review Press, 1973) 298.

15. Jordan, 41-52.

16. Wilcom E. Washburn, *The Indian and the Whiteman* (New York: Anchor Books, 1964) 101-36; Jordan, 27.

17. Thomas F. Gossett, *Race: The History of an Idea in America* (New York: Schocken Books, 1965) 48.

18. Gossett, *Race* 46.

essentially inferior to whites.[19] The ideological rationale for slavery and white racial dominance over nonwhite peoples developed even more under the attacks of the antislavery forces in America and Britain. (These were the social forces that contributed to the movement for racial unity, which we will discuss later.)

In the 1760s, a "paper war" broke out between the slave lobby and the anti-slavery forces. The former maintained (as did their American counterparts) that blacks were an inferior species. The latter, sometimes to the detriment of blacks, maintained the counterbelief that blacks were "innocent child[ren] of nature."[20] Unfortunately, the proslavery forces in both countries had more influential people supporting them. David Hume, the Scottish philosopher and historian, contributed greatly to the development of ideological racism when he remarked:

> I am apt to suspect the Negro to be naturally inferior to the white. There never was a civilized nation of any other complexion than white, or even any individual eminent either in action or speculation. No ingenious manu-facturer among them, no arts, no sciences. There are Negro slaves dispersed all over Europe, of which none ever discovered any symptom of ingenuity.[21]

Similar views were expressed across the Atlantic by Jefferson and other influential white Americans. Jefferson, however, played a major role in foster-ing ideological racism in America during the formative years of white America's thinking on race and the place of blacks within the American Grand Experience.

---

19.   Gossett, *Race* 44.

20.   Walvin, 21.

21.   Quoted in Walvin, 21.

CHAPTER 3

THOMAS JEFFERSON'S VIEW OF
A MULTIRACIAL AMERICA

I advance it, therefore, as a suspicion only, that the blacks, whether originally a distinct race, or made distinct by time and circumstances, are inferior to the whites in the endowment both of body and mind.

Thomas Jefferson

Thomas Jefferson was not only a slave owner like his contemporary George Washington and others among the "founding fathers," but, unlike many of them, Jefferson was also a man of letters whose writings influenced generations of Americans and Europeans. As two scholars of Jefferson have pointed out: "No leader in the period of the American Enlightenment was as articulate, as wise, as conscious of the implications and consequences of free society as he."[1] That being the case, Jefferson wielded enormous influence on the thinking of his age in the areas of science and politics, but especially, in race relations. What he thought and wrote about race was key to the thinking of future American generations. "In the years after the Revolution the speculations of Thomas Jefferson were of great importance because so many people read and reacted to them," another scholar wrote. "His remarks about Negroes in the only book he ever wrote were more widely read, in all probability, than any others until the mid-nineteenth century."[2] Unfortunately, Thomas Jefferson, one of America's greatest leaders and thinkers, was also one of the first Americans to formulate an ideology of racism, particularly antiblack racism. In short, Thomas Jefferson was the first among America's ideological racists.

The scholar of American racism finds in Thomas Jefferson's life and writings many racial phobias and beliefs that still plague contemporary white America. Jefferson worried about slavery much as many contemporary white Americans worry about racism and the plight of the black community: solely in regard to its impact on the whites. Like many contemporary white Americans, Jefferson harbored racist beliefs about blacks. He feared black uprisings and entertained all kinds of notions about black sexuality. He firmly believed in the superiority of whites over blacks. According to Jefferson, blacks and whites could never co-exist on equal terms in America. These views were incorporated in his *Notes on the State of Virginia*, written between 1781-82. No one can say that Jefferson was not concerned about the evils and social and historical consequences of slavery upon American society. He was among the first to recognize

---

1.   Adrienne Koch and William Peden, *The Life and Selected Writings of Thomas Jefferson* (New York: Modern Library, 1944) xv.

2.   Jordan, 165.

the costs of slavery on the moral and psychological development of white children even as he neglected to articulate fully slavery's deadening effects upon the body, mind, and souls of generations of black slaves and their descendants. Of the effects on whites, he wrote:

> There must doubtless be an unhappy influence on the manners of our people produced by the existence of slavery among us. The whole commerce between master and slave is a perpetual exercise of the most boisterous passions, the most unremitting despotism on our part, and degrading submissions on the other. Our children see this and learn to imitate it. . . .From his cradle to his grave he is learning to do what he sees others do. If a parent could find no motive either in his philanthropy or his self-love, for restraining the intemperance of passion towards his slave, it should always be a sufficient one that his child is present. . . .The parent storms, the child looks on, catches the lineaments of wrath, puts on the same airs in the circle of smaller slaves, gives loose to the worst of passions, and thus nursed, educated, and daily exercised in tyranny, cannot but be stamped by it with odious peculiarities. The man must be a prodigy who can retain his manners and morals undepraved by such circumstances.[3]

Jefferson could see the pathology of racial dominance inherent in slavery and how it affected white children. He reveals the process by which white Americans reared under slavery developed their sense of racial superiority. He was obviously very concerned for the moral and psychological health of white children. The effects of their racism on black children, within that "circle of smaller slaves," is mentioned only parenthetically, clearly a shadow issue in Jefferson's mind. Slavery destroys not only the morals of a people but also their industry, as Jefferson remarked:

> With the morals of the people, their industry also is destroyed. For in a warm climate, no man will labor for himself who can make another labor for him. This is so true, that of the proprietors of slaves a very small proportion indeed are ever seen to labor. And can the liberties of a nation be thought secure when we have removed their only firm basis, a conviction in the minds of the people that these liberties are the gift of God? That they are not to be violated but with His wrath?[4]

The costs of slavery, then, weighed heavily on white slaveholders. The greatest cost, perhaps, was their disinclination to work. "No man will labor for himself who can make another labor for him." Slavery, then, not only distorted the hearts and souls of whites who held them but also destroyed the sanctity of labor itself, or at least the hard, difficult, backbreaking labor that the slaves were forced to do on behalf of whites. As bothersome as these costs of slavery

---

3. Koch and Peden, 278.

4. Koch and Peden, 278-79.

were to Jefferson, he worried more about a great possible cost to America exacted by God for the crime of slavery. That cost might possibly come in the shape of black rebellions, which Jefferson and most planters who owned slaves constantly feared.

> Indeed I tremble for my country when I reflect that God is just; that his justice cannot sleep forever; that considering numbers, nature and natural means only, a revolution of the wheel of fortune, an exchange of situation is among possible events: that it may become probable by supernatural interference! The almighty has no attribute which can take side with us in such a contest.[5]

Jefferson lived long enough to see his worst fears of God's wrath realized, but happily for him and his fellow white Americans, in another region, Haiti. Haiti had been under French rule until black slaves under the leadership of a black military genius (Toussaint l'Ouverture) defeated Napoleon's troops in a two-year bloody war that ended in 1793 with the black slaves gaining their freedom.[6] To Jefferson, this revolt of black slaves was only the first chapter. "If something is not done," he warned, "we shall be the murderers of our own children."[7] Here again, Jefferson was calculating the great cost whites would have to pay if they did not free black slaves. Jefferson spent much of his life agonizing over the issue of slavery. But that agony did not prevent him from contributing his considerable share to racist thought in America.

Thomas Jefferson's views on blacks were among the most racist of his time. Some would say that he reflected his time, that he was shaped by the slave-holding culture of which he was but a part. While such an explanation is certainly true to some extent, it fails to account for the tremendous intellectual efforts Jefferson devoted to demeaning blacks as human beings. Jefferson seemed to have gone out of his way in his efforts to prove that blacks were inferior to whites. It is in this context that we must regard him as the premier ideological racist of his day. Jefferson not only believed that blacks were inferior but also that they could never join white Americans as equals in the Great Republic.

> It will probably be asked, why not retain and incorporate the blacks into the State? Deep-rooted prejudices entertained by the whites; ten thousand recollections, by the blacks, of the injuries they have sustained; new provocations; the real distinctions which nature has made; and many other circumstances, will divide us into parties, and produce convulsions, which will probably never end except in the extermination of the one or the other race. To these objections, which are political, may be added others, which are physical and

---

5.   Koch and Peden, 279.

6.   C.L.R. James, *The Black Jacobins: Toussaint Louverture and the San Dominigo Reveloution* (New York: First Vintage Edition, 1963) iv.

7.   Jordon, 169.

moral. The first difference which strikes us is that of color. Is this difference of no importance? Is it not the foundation of a greater or lesser share of beauty in the two races?[8]

Jefferson made a strong case for not incorporating blacks into the body politic. The prejudices of whites and the recollections of blacks would be, it seemed to him, too volatile, too irreconcilable. On this point, we can perhaps sympathize with Jefferson. He had few if any examples of multiracial societies in which former black slaves and their former white masters had come together on an equal basis to build a nation. At this juncture of modern history with all its potential for great human glory and tragedy, even the greatest visionaries found difficulty incorporating a peoplehood of black, red, and white. Few such visions transcended the pervasive ethnocentric views of the English-turned-Americans who still struggled with the perjorative meaning of blackness lodged in their innermost being. Jefferson not only had difficulty envisioning blacks and whites sharing a common country on an equal basis, he also had difficulty imagining that blacks could ever be as beautiful as whites.

Are not the fine mixtures of red and white, the expressions of color in the one, preferable to that eternal monotony, which reigns in the countenances, that immovable veil of black which covers the emotions of the other races? Add to these, flowing hair, a more elegant symetry of form, their own judgement in favor of the whites, declared by their preference of them, as uniformly as is the preference of the Orangutan for the black women over his own species. . . .[9]

Continuing, Jefferson points to more differences between blacks and whites, which he contends separate blacks and whites. Blacks "seem to require less sleep. A black, after hard labor through the day, will be induced by the slightest amusement to sit up till midnight, or later, though knowing he must be out with first dawn of the morning." It did not not seem to occur to Jefferson that black slaves had to have a life of their own whenever they could get it. He could only see from a white planter's point of view, namely, that slaves should work hard all day then sleep as much as they could so they would be able to work harder for the master. At one point when he credited blacks with being "—at least as brave, and more adventuresome" than whites, he quickly added, "But this may perhaps proceed from a want of forethought, which prevents their seeing a danger till it be present." Of black love and affection, Jefferson had this to say: "They are more ardent after their female; but love seems with them to be more an eager desire, than a tender delicate mixture of sentiment and sensations." And of black grief, "Their griefs are transient. Those numberless afflictions, which render it doubtful whether heaven has given life to us in mercy or in

---

8.   Koch and Peden, 256.

9 .   Koch and Peden, 256.

wrath, are less felt, and sooner forgotten with them." In addition, the general state of blacks, Jefferson believed, was little more than an existence that "—appears to participate more of sensation than reflection. To this must be ascribed their disposition to sleep when abstracted from their diversions, and unemployed in labor."[10]

One can readily see how Jefferson became the premier ideological racist of his day. He seemed unwilling to recognize the slightest indication of black humanity. Blacks could not be brave and more adventuresome without being seen by Jefferson as lacking forethought. The love of the black man for the black women was too ardent for Jefferson's taste "more an eager desire, than a tender delicate mixture of sentiment and sensation." Of all of Jefferson's views of blacks, his views of black male sexuality revealed the deep-rooted fears and anxieties of generations of white males.[11] As a slaveowner who more than once commented on the tragic effects of slavery on whites, Jefferson did not seem overly concerned with the burden of slavery upon his black slaves. He tended to trivilalize their grief as "transient," which he thought "soon forgotten with them." Adding much insult to injury, he then reduced their general existence to little more than that of "sensation" rather than of "reflection."

This was not all Jefferson had to say about blacks. He made a greater contribution to racist thought in America with his comments on black mental inferiority. It is in this area that Jefferson, the founding father of white America, paved the way for a strand of racism which still works to poison the soul of white America and to divide it from black America. Jordan places the blame squarely on Jefferson's shoulders: "Of far more import for the Negro's future were Jefferson's remarks on mental capacity. More than any other single person he framed the terms of the debate still carried on today."[12] Jefferson not only "framed the terms of the debate still carried on today," he also provided generations of white Americans with an intellectual defense of white racism. Indeed,

---

10. Jefferson's fears and anxieties concerning black male sexuality became such an obsession that he once proposed a bill to the Virginia legislature to require a white woman who had borne a child by a black man to leave the state or be placed beyond the protection of the law. See, John Chester Miller, *The Wolf by the Ears: Thomas Jefferson and Slavery* (New York: Free Press, 1977) 64.

11. White male fear of black male/white female sexual relations has played a major role in the psychohistorical development of racial attitudes in the larger white society going back to the earliest contacts between the English and the Africans, Jordon, 18-22. This phobia on the part of southern white males assumed pathological proportions during the post-emancipation period when white males felt that they were losing control of black males. They responded by inventing a mental image of the black former-slave as "beast-rapist," "insatiable satyr," out to get the fair damsels of the South. See, Joel Williamson, *A Rage for Order: Black-White Relations in the American South Since Emancipation* (New York: Oxford University Press, 1986) 186-91. For some insights into how this sexual-racial phobia manifests itself in present-day American society, see, Bob Blauner, *Black Lives, White Lives: Three Decades of Race Relations in America* (Berkeley: University of California, 1989) 247-48.

12. Jordan, 171.

this following quotation gave Jefferson the historical distinction of being a founding father of the most popular and oldest school of racist thought in America:

> Comparing them by their faculties of memory, reason, and imagination, it appears to me that in memory they are equal to the whites; in reason much inferior, as I think one could scarcely be found capable of tracing and comprehending the investigations of Euclid; and that in imagination they are dull, tasteless, anomalous. It would be unfair to follow them to Africa for this investigation. We will consider them here, on the same stage with the whites, and where the facts are not apocryphal on which a judgment is to be formed. It will be right to make great allowances for the differences of condition, of education, of conversation, of the sphere in which they move. Many millions of them have been brought to, and born in America. Most of them, indeed, have been confined to tillage, to their own homes, and their own society; yet many have been so situated, that they might have availed themselves of the conversations of their masters. Many have been brought up to the handicraft arts, and from that circumstance have always been associated with the whites. Some have been liberally educated, and all have lived in countries where the arts and sciences are cultivated to a considerable degree, and all have had before their eyes samples of the best works. The Indian, with no advantage of this kind, will often carve figures on their pages not destitute of design and merit. They will crayon out an animal, a plant, or a country, so as to prove the existence of a germ in their minds which only wants cultivation. They astonish you with strokes of the most sublime-oratory; such as prove their reason and sentiment strong, their imagination growing and elevated. But never yet could I find that a black had uttered a thought above the level of plain narration; never saw even an elementary trait of painting or sculpture. In music they are more generally gifted than the whites with accurate ears for tune and time. Whether they will be equal to the composition of a more extensive run of melody, or of complicated harmony, is yet to be proved.[13]

Jefferson's analysis of blacks' mental abilities as compared to whites and Indians revealed the emergence of an historical pattern of white ideological racism that would persist for many generations. Anti-environmentalism formed the crux of this historical pattern of racist thought. Basically, it argued that no amount of opportunity or exposure could alter the mental capacity of blacks. They were, by nature, inferior. Even the Indians, who lacked the so-called advantages of blacks, could do better. By focusing on the carefully contrived deficits of blacks within equally contrived situations in which they should have been able to demonstrate great ability but failed to do so, Jefferson was able to give the impression that he was measuring both blacks and Indian with the same stick. But Jefferson was committed to rationalizing his racist interpretation of blacks by any means at his disposal for the simple reason that to fail to do so would place the total burden of racial guilt upon white society. Here

---

13. Koch and Peden, 257-58.

again, he was among the first American ideological racists to use this method of victim-blaming to deflect blame away from a system of white racial oppression.

Comparing black efforts to great Indian achievements despite lack of advantages supposedly available to blacks was another device employed by Jefferson to blame blacks for their condition. Although both blacks and Indians suffered at the hands of white Americans, Jefferson chose to place Indians on a more equal basis with whites than he did blacks. In fact, he once even stated that Indians were the equals in intelligence and morality to whites. Unlike his intense negative feelings toward blacks' physical attributes, he found the color of Indians close to that of Mediterranean Europeans. In contrast to his views of black-white intermixture, Jefferson, much like many other contemporary whites, accepted racial mixing between whites and Indians while rejecting similar mixing between blacks and whites. He was proud of the fact that both of his daughters had married descendants of Pocahontas and that the blood of Indian royalty therefore flowed in the veins of his grandchildren. In Jefferson's view, racial unity was possible but only between whites and Indians. Addressing the Indians on this subject, he stated, "Your blood will mix with ours and will spread with ours over this great land," until white and Indian become one people and one nation. The Indian, therefore, in contrast to the black, was in Jefferson's view a Noble Savage.[14]

To return to Jefferson's use—or more accurately put, misuse—of the contrast of blacks and Indians in relation to white America, this device of comparing blacks with other ethnic groups so as to deflect attention and blame away from the historical costs and consequences of white racial oppression upon black people has been used repeatedly by white Americans. As we have seen and as other scholars of Jefferson's racial views have noticed, Jefferson "seemed incapable of complimenting Negroes without immediately adding qualifications."[15] This racial tendency would also be transmitted down countless white generations to the present day. Blacks were good at music with some qualification but probably not good at more complicated musical forms. Although blacks were overly burdened with misery, which Jefferson commented is "often the parent of the most affecting touches in poetry," he snatched from blacks even the mind and spirit to produce good poetry from their misery: "Among the blacks is misery enough, God knows, but no poetry. Love is the peculiar oestrum of the poet. Their love is ardent, but it kindles the senses only, not the imagination."[16] As for the famous black-American poet Phyllis Wheatly, born in Africa and brought to America as a small child and reared by a wealthy white Boston family, and who published her first poem in 1770,[17] she was simply not good enough to alter Jefferson's views of

---

14. Quoted in Miller, 65.

15. Jordan, 172.

16. Koch and Peden, 258-59.

17. John Hope Franklin, *From Slavery to Freedom: A History of Negro America,* 4th ed. (New York: Alfred A. Knopf, 1974) 87.

black inferiority. "Religion, indeed, has produced a Phyllis Whately [*sic*]," he conceded, "but it could not produce a poet. The compositions published under her name are below the dignity of criticism."[18]

Phyllis Wheatly's work had impressed some of Jefferson's contemporaries, such as George Washington and Voltaire, and five editions of her book of poetry were published before 1800. In addition, she translated segments of Ovid, which should have impressed Jefferson even more given his classical orientation. She received much acclaim in England from a host of nobles, including Lord Dartmouth, and when she returned to Boston, the *Gazette* sounded a rousing welcome for her in its pages, calling her "the extraordinary Poetical Genius."[19] But Jefferson was still too encumbered with his racist views to allow even these achievements to persuade him to appreciate this first great black poet in America.

However, Jefferson was trying in his own unique way to understand his views concerning blacks. Benjamin Banneker, a free black from Maryland, known for his achievements as a mathematician, astronomer, and a clockmaker, forced Jefferson to modify some of his racist beliefs concerning blacks, even though Jefferson continued to cling to most such beliefs even after acknowledging Banneker's great achievements. In 1791, Banneker sent Jefferson a manuscript of an almanac he had put together. No doubt aware of Jefferson's and some of his contemporaries' antiblack biases, Banneker informed Jefferson in no uncertain terms that he hoped Jefferson would see the manuscript as the long soughtafter evidence of what blacks could achieve. He went on to comment that he had heard that Jefferson was friendly towards blacks, therefore, he believed that Jefferson, as the author of the Declaration of Independence, would be open to proof of achievement regardless of race. But, Banneker was not finished with Jefferson. He then proceeded to chastise Jefferson for violating his principles by holding slaves in a state of "tyrannical thralldom and inhuman captivity," and of being insensitive to the "cruel oppression" of thousands of blacks. Then Banneker reminded Jefferson of how different the present state of affairs was from the days of 1776 when people were committed to eliminating every trace of oppression.[20] Jefferson accepted both the manuscript and the scolding from Banneker. In his reply, Jefferson demonstrated his respect for Banneker's feelings and some indications that the manuscript provided the long-awaited proof that blacks were quite capable of remarkable achievements:

> Sir, - I thank you sincerely for your letter of the 19th instant, and for the Almanac it contained. Nobody wishes more than I do to see such proofs as you exhibit, that nature has given to our black brethren, talents equal to those of the other colors of men, and that the appearance of a want of them is owing merely to the degraded condition of their condition, both in Africa

18.   Koch and Peden, 259.

19.   Quoted in Miller, 75-76.

20.   Miller, 76.

and America. I can add with truth, that nobody wishes more ardently to see a good system commenced for raising the condition both of their body and mind to what it ought to be, as fast as the imbecility of their present existence, and other circumstances which cannot be neglected, will admit. I have taken the liberty of sending your Almanac to Monsieur de Condorcet, Secretary of the Academy of Science at Paris, and member of the Philanthropic Society, because I considered it as a document to which your color had a right for their justification against the doubts which have been entertained of them. I am, with great esteem, sir, Your most obedient humble servant.[21]

In his cover letter to Banneker's Almanac sent to the Marquis de Condorcet, Jefferson expressed his delight and approval that it was possible for a black man to become a very respectful mathematician who could produce "very elegant solutions of Geometrical problems." However, Jefferson could not avoid his tendency to place qualifications once again on Banneker's achievements. According to Jefferson, Banneker's great achievements did not, as Banneker desired, furnish proof that blacks if given a chance were capable of achieving as much as whites. Banneker was only an exception. While agreeing in part that Banneker's achievements were impressive, Jefferson was too influenced by his own racism to see blacks as ever being equal to whites, no matter how much individual blacks achieved. "I shall be delighted to see these instances of moral eminence so multiplied as to prove that the want of talents observed in them, is merely the effects of their degraded conditions, and not proceeding from any difference in the structure of the parts on which the intellect depends."[22]

It is important to note that Jefferson was reflecting a cultural tendency that would come to characterize certain kinds of prejudiced patterns of thinking among white Americans. In cases where racism is so deep that to uproot it would cause prejudiced people great emotional upheaval by forcing them to change their view of the world radically, these people engage in countless qualifications—what the late Gordon Allport described as "refencing." Allport's explanation is very helpful in understanding Jefferson's tendency to place qualifications on black achievements:

> For our purposes it is important to understand what happens when categories conflict with evidence. . . .It is a striking fact that in most instances categories are stubborn and resist change. After all, we have fashioned our generalizations as we have because they have worked fairly well. Why change them to accommodate every new bit of evidence? To do so would only disturb our satisfactory set of habits. We selectively admit new evidence to a category if it confirms us in our previous belief. . . .But if we find evidence that is contradictory to our preconceptions, we are likely to grow resistant. There is a common mental device that permits people to hold to

---

21. Koch and Peden, 508-9.

22. Quoted in Miller, 76.

prejudgments even in the face of much contradictory evidence. It is the device of admitting exceptions. . . .By excluding a few favored cases, the negative rubic is kept intact for all cases. In short, contrary evidence is not admitted and allowed to modify the generalization. . . .Let us call this the "refencing device." When a fact cannot fit into a mental field, the exception is acknowledged, but the field is hastily fenced in again and not allowed to remain dangerously open.[23]

In the case of Banneker and other exceptional blacks, Jefferson and those of his contemporaries who shared his racist views of blacks, would find the use of refencing critical to the maintenance and perpetuation of ideological racism. Future generations of whites would employ this device almost unconsciously in their attempts to avoid confronting their antiblack prejudices. Some whites, however, placed no such qualifications upon black achievement. While Banneker was most certainly an exceptional black, in their eyes he was also an example of what the black race as a whole was capable of achieving if given a chance. James McHenry, who later became Secretary of War in the cabinet of John Adams and who assisted Banneker in obtaining important contacts within the national government, took the opposite position from Hume and Jefferson, who might on occasion accept the accomplishments of "rare" blacks but remained convinced that the majority of blacks were still inferior to the majority of whites. McHenry did not engage in such refencing. To him, Banneker represented "fresh proof that the powers of the mind are disconnected with the color of the skin, or, in other words, a striking contradiction to Mr. Hume's doctrine, that the Negroes are naturally inferior to the whites, and unsusceptible of attainments in arts and science."[24] McHenry was not alone in his rejection of the antiblack views of Hume, Jefferson, and others. When Banneker arrived in the District of Columbia to take up his duties, the *Georgetown Weekly Ledger* contradicted Jefferson's qualified acceptance of Banneker as proof of what blacks could do by describing him as "an Ethiopian whose abilities as surveyor and astronomer already prove that Mr. Jefferson's concluding that that race of men were void of mental endowment was without foundation."[25]

In all fairness to Jefferson, he did assist Banneker in obtaining a job as a surveyor in the District of Columbia where the new federal city was to be located. But Jefferson paid a dear price for even corresponding with Banneker. When his first letter to Banneker appeared in print, Jefferson found himself in serious political trouble. Although he still harbored antiblack prejudices that he would take to his grave, Jefferson had violated sacred southern mores by writing to a black man and calling blacks, "his black brethren." As his party's candidate for

23.   Gordon Allport. *The Nature of Prejudice* (Massachusetts: Addison-Wesley Publishing Company, 1954) 23.

24.   Quoted in Franklin, 89.

25.   Quoted in Franklin, 89.

president in 1796, Jefferson was taken to task by an avowed racist, William Smith, a South Carolina Federalist. "What shall we think of a secretary of state thus fraternizing with Negroes, writing them complimentary epistles, styling them his black brethren, congratulating them on the evidences of their genius, and assuring them of his good wishes for their speedy emancipation."[26] Jefferson lost the presidency to John Adams by a margin of three votes in the electoral college. He had paid a high price for even his qualified acceptance of individual black achievements and limited future possibilities. "Thus it was borne in upon Jefferson," according to a scholar of Jefferson's views on slavery, "that the course of political wisdom was to ignore the blacks and the problems they created. . . .Expediency dictated that slavery be treated as though somehow, sometime, and by means as yet undisclosed, it would go away of its own accord."[27]

Over time, this self-serving attitude of Jefferson and other members of the slave-holding class created greater and greater costs. The moral compromise over slavery eroded the very spirit of white planters who, as Jefferson had pointed out, would not labor as long as they had someone to labor for them. Slavery also necessitated the brutalization of blacks and created the need to demean them systematically in both their own eyes and the eyes of white society. With blacks as slaves and important founding fathers as slave owners and articulate ideologues of white supremacy, few Americans could envision a multiracial society based on justice, equality, and racial unity. Only the Quakers came close to this vision of a racially unified America.[28] Jefferson and the majority of white Americans could only see the forceful expansion of white civilization over the land and bodies of red peoples with black people somewhere tucked away from sight or better yet, emancipated from slavery and shipped away to their African or Haitian homelands.

Whatever grand legacy Jefferson left to future generations of Americans and the world, the vision of a multiracial society where peoples from all racial backgrounds could live in justice and peace was not part of this legacy. Jefferson, as did so many of his contemporaries, believed first and foremost in the establishment of a white nation, with whites in charge, fulfilling their spiritual destiny. As much as Jefferson enjoyed looking into the future of America, he could not envision an America where blacks and whites lived on terms of equality. "Nothing is more certainly written in the book of fate," he wrote in his autobiography, "than that the two races, equally free, cannot live in the same government. Nature, habit, opinions have drawn indelible lines of distinction between them."[29] Driven by his twin fears of racial war and miscegenation between blacks and whites, Jefferson and many of his contemporaries could only see a

---

26. Quoted in Miller, 78.

27. Miller, 78.

28. Jordan, 139-40.

29. Quoted in Miller, 278.

white America achieved through the gradual emancipation and relocation of blacks far "beyond the reach of mixture." To this end, Jefferson supported the efforts of the American Colonization Society organized in 1816 to remove free blacks from American soil to any place where they would not come into contact with whites. The plan failed because of numerous reasons, including the cost of transporting blacks as their numbers increased, the refusal of many free blacks to abandon a place that they considered their home, and other organizational problems.[30]

Jefferson, desperate to get rid of blacks so that white America could get on with its business of spreading white civilization over the Western hemisphere, even proposed separating black children from their parents, training and supporting the children as wards of the State until they were ready to live on their own, and then shipping them to Africa or any other convenient place away from contact with whites. The remaining older blacks would then simply die off naturally, and America's racial problem would be solved. Such a desperate proposal by Jefferson moved one historian to comment: "That Thomas Jefferson, by nature a kindhearted, benevolent, well-intentioned man, should have recommended such a draconian method for attaining the 'beatitude' of an all-white society reveals how urgent he deemed it to be to separate physically the two races." Unable or unwilling to envision racial unity among blacks and whites, Jefferson, was determined to "dispose of an unassimilable and potentially dangerous race which, in his opinion, endangered the peace, well-being, and racial purity of the American people."[31]

Notwithstanding his other great accomplishments, Jefferson contributed to the development of the evils of racism in America. He could have made a contribution to the vision of racial unity—like Benjamin Rush and scores of Quakers—but he could see only a white America. A year before he died in 1826, Jefferson was visited by Lafayette, who had not been to America since 1784. The latter was shocked by many of the changes that had occurred. But, the most startling change was the increase in racial prejudice. He sadly but accurately concluded that the American Revolution had benefitted only white

---

30. Miller, 264-71; Several major white American leaders were unable to conceive of a multiracial society where whites were not in total control of blacks. They could not envision racial unity between blacks and whites. Even Abraham Lincoln, the "Great Emancipator," labored to get rid of blacks so as to achieve a white-only America. See, Charles H. Wesley, "Lincoln's Plan for Colonizing the Emancipated Negroes," *The Journal of Negro History* 4 (January 1919): 2-21; most free blacks rejected white leaders' attempts to colonize them because blacks felt that they had contributed to the development of America. In this sense, one could argue that these blacks played a key role in shaping the vision of America as a multiracial society. For black Americans' views on African colonization and their role in the future of America, see: Bella Gross, "The First National Negro Convention," *The Journal of Negro History* 41 (October, 1946): 435-43; Louis R. Mehlinger, "The Attitude of the Free Negro toward African Colonization," *The Journal of Negro History* 1 (July, 1916): 276-301.

31. Miller, 271.

men.[32]

At this stage of American race relations—the stage of shaping the image of blacks in the American white mind—it is crucial to understand the psycho-historical aspects of Jefferson's views of blacks. In many ways Jefferson reflected the evolving white views of the black presence. Confronted by the enormity of the contradiction of enslaving a people while advocating freedom and building a nation (for whites mainly and perhaps Indians if they conformed), Jefferson and generations of whites after him would simply and systematically rationalize their oppression of black slaves. They would consciously and unconsciously nurture the seed of white-skin privilege, of the unquestioned rights of whites to conquer and rule nonwhite peoples not only in America but also throughout the world. The human cost of this lack of interracial vision led to the continuation of slavery with its attendant evils of racial hatred and fear and to a sectional conflict that triggered a bloody civil war which cost thousands of lives. Worse still, the racial ramifications of that war and its subsequent historical developments of segregation, race riots, racial fear, and hatred still poison the core of America's national life and culture.

---

32. Miller, 273-74.

Part II

Barriers to Racial Unity and Multiracial Progress

CHAPTER 4

WHITE MANIFEST DESTINY
AND THE VICTIMIZATION
OF NATIVE AND AFRICAN PEOPLES

> Humanity has often wept over the fate of the aborigines of this country, and
> philanthropy has been long busily employed in devising means to avert it,
> but its progress has never for a moment been arrested, and one by one have
> many powerful tribes disappeared from the earth. To follow to the tomb the
> last of his race and tread on the graves of extinct nations excite melancholy
> reflections. But true philanthropy reconciles the mind to these vicissitudes
> as it does to the extinction of one generation to make room for another.
>
> President Andrew Jackson
> Second Annual Message to Congress, 1830

Lost Opportunities for Building a Multiracial
Society Based on Harmony and Justice

The greatest historical cost of the European conquest and development of
America was the systematic victimization and dehumanization of the Native
and African peoples. We will never know what kind of multiracial society
America would have been had those Europeans who chose the historical track
of conquest and slavery over peoples of color instead chosen the historical track
leading to racial unity, love, and fellowship. We can only wonder at what great
material and spiritual achievements would have been possible had the other
track been chosen. Centuries of bloodshed and hatred would have been
avoided. The tremendous energy channelled into the conquest of the Native
peoples and the enslavement of Africans could have gone into developing
methods of greater and greater cooperation among all racial groups, cooperation
that in turn would have released and channeled the combined cultural and spiritual talents of African, Indian, and European peoples to build one of the greatest
human civilizations in the history of the human species.

Had this historical convergence of different races and peoples been energized
by some great spiritual force sweeping the world, there would have been a
tremendous synergistic revolution in human material and spiritual relationships.
The entire world would have been spared much racial strife, but this convergence of peoples occurred during the time of European expansion and conquest,
when human greed was fast overtaking the quest for spiritual growth and development. Several centuries would have to pass before people would understand
the connection between racial unity and social progress and to have sufficient
spiritual guidance to make a choice. At the time of the great European discov-
eries and conquests, minds were turned to gold, silver, lands, and great

adventures, at the expense of non-European peoples. Social progress came to mean white manifest destiny.

It is so easy and always tempting to look back over history and engage in endless speculation about what could have happened if only we had done such and such, much like the proverbial Monday-morning quarterback who relives the Great Game that took place over the past weekend. However, if we as human beings living in a world where conflict and violence have become common fixtures of our daily lives do not look back over the Great Games of human experience and learn from them, we, as George Santayana put it, "who cannot remember the past are condemned to repeat it." The history of racial contacts between Europeans on one side and Native and African peoples on the other side embodies profound lessons for the entire human race. Understanding these lessons is all the more important in the wake of the preparation for the upcoming five-hundredth anniversary of Columbus's first voyage to the so-called New World. As governments and historical societies throughout the Western world celebrate this historic event, many questions will surface concerning the historical lessons learned since the time Columbus first landed in the Americas.

Depending on one's historical and futuristic perspectives on the "meaning" of human history in the fullest sense of the term, the last 500 years can be interpreted in many ways. Most certainly, one must acknowledge the traditional interpretations that focus on the European exploration of the Western Hemisphere, exploration that led to the rise and development of African slavery within the world system of capitalism, along with the emergence of semi-democratic State systems. For our purposes, however, the most significant aspect of this period is that it witnessed the historical convergence of peoples from very distinct racial and cultural backgrounds, albeit within very tragic and far-reaching historical circumstances: the European extermination of several indigenous peoples and cultures and the enslavement of Africans.

This process of systematic victimization was no historical aberration of European exploration and settlement of the Western Hemisphere. Rather, it evolved as a direct consequence of the emergence of the European world economic system. While this world economic system provided the historical and structural context in which European and Non-European peoples in the Western Hemisphere first established contact, the nature and direction of these first formative multiracial contacts were in many ways predetermined by a set of culturally based perceptions and values Europeans brought with them to the New World. Foremost among these perceptions and values was the notion that they, as Europeans, were a chosen people with a destiny that included the expansion of their "European Christian Civilization" over the face of the earth. Non-Europeans had no vote in the matter. One such theory, called by some historians, "the European theory of the right of discovery," grew out of an ancient claim by Christians that they had the right to dispossess non-Christians of their land anywhere in the world. This theory was reinforced by an even more ethnocentric theory transformed into tradition called *vacuum domicilium*, which "held that land, not 'occupied' or 'settled' was available to any 'civilized' person—that is Christian—who, of course, had the exclusive right to determine whether or not a land was 'settled'."[1]

These two views sanctioned the right of European Christians to dispossess the Native peoples in the New World of their land. But, another European view that further eroded the possibility of building a just and harmonious multiracial society in the New World was the "idea that someone else should do the hard manual work of the world," namely Indians or Africans. This view, according to one scholar of race relations in the New World, "appealed strongly to sixteenth-century Spaniards, who inherited a taste for martial glory and religious conquest and a distaste for physical labor from their medieval forefathers who had struggled for centuries to free Spain from the Moslem."[2] While the Spaniards were prepared to fight to the death to plant their flag, serve their king, and advance Christianity, "they were not prepared, however, to settle down as farmers to till the soil or as miners to extract gold and silver from the bowels of the earth. That was work for Indians."[3] When adequate Indian labor was not available, the Spaniards were dumbfounded and complained to the king. It was inconceivable that they themselves should do such work. At one point in the colonial history of Spanish America, the town officials of Buenos Aires were forced by circumstances to inform the king "affairs were so bad there that Spaniards actually had to dig in the earth and plant crops if they were to eat." In still another case, Spaniards reported how they had seen their fellow Spaniards die of hunger and others working in the fields with "their own hands"—something these observers had never before witnessed. [4]

This negative view of labor came to dominate the thinking of Spaniards and other Europeans throughout the New World and in most areas of the world in which Europeans colonized non-Europeans.[5] "Throughout the whole of the colonial period and all the lands colonized by Spain," Lewis Hanke has written, "this same attitude prevailed. . . ."[6] These views of labor and work became linked to race and culture soon after the Europeans began their conquest of the New World. This historical linkage determined in large part the future of race relations in the Americas. In short, it was part of the first set of barriers placed

1.   Forrest G. Wood, *The Arrogance of Faith: Christianity and Race in America from the Colonial Era to the Twentieth Century* (New York: Alfred A. Knopf, 1990) 217.

2.   Lewis Hanke, *Aristotle and the American Indians* (Bloomington: Indiana University Press, 1959) 13.

3.   Hanke, 14. Africans later were enslaved to do this work.

4.   Hanke, 14.

5.   For an analysis of some aspects of this historical relationship between European use of the labor of non-European people, see "White Capital and Colored Labor" in E. Franklin Frazier, *Race and Culture Contacts in the Modern World* (Boston: Beacon Press, 1957) 127-56.

6.   Hanke, 14.

in the path of genuine racial unity and cooperation between European and Native peoples. The philosophical rationale of the linkage was provided by the Aristotelian doctrine of natural slavery.

The Aristotelian doctrine of natural slavery, which argued some human beings were set apart by nature to serve others, appealed to many Europeans seeking ways to exploit the vast mineral and human resources of the New World.[7] John Major, a Scottish professor in Paris, helped pave the way for the application of this doctrine to the Indians of the New World. He was not only the first to apply the doctrine of natural slavery to Indians, he also supported the idea that force against the Indians should be used in preparation to teaching them Christianity. His views were published in 1510.[8] One can readily see how such racial views would contaminate the relationships between peoples from different cultures and destroy or delay any attempt to build a multiracial society based on justice.

Without being an incorrigible optimist, one could still argue that even with all the racial-cultural baggage European colonizers brought with them, options for creating a multiracial society based upon justice and cooperation were still possible at various historical points of the encounters of Native peoples, Africans, and Europeans. But given the perceptions, values, and power of the Europeans in this historical drama, such an idea was not attractive. As any other people might have been under similar circumstances, European colonizers of the New World were beside themselves with cultural arrogance. Their so-called discovery of the New World was intoxicating. Some Europeans found it difficult not to think that they were indeed "God's gift to the world." Not even the universal ideas of the Enlightenment and the American Revolution could stem the tide of racial pride among certain European groups. By the time Joseph Arthur de Gobineau published his famous book on the inequality of the human races in 1854, he was merely "summarizing and amplifying more than half a century of ideas on race rather than inaugurating a new era."[9] The seeds of those racial ideas were sown centuries earlier.

The English brought with them a special brand of racial enthnocentrism that in contact with Native and African peoples grew into a systematic form of racial dominance supported by an equally systematic theological and "scientific" rationalization. The English arrived and began their conquest of America with the notion that they had a divine racial right to rule over both the land and the people. As historian Reginald Horseman explained it:

Although the concept of a distinct, superior Anglo-Saxon race, with innate endowments enabling it to achieve a perfection of governmental institutions

---

7.   Hanke, 14.

8.   Hanke, 14.

9.   Reginald Horseman, *Race and Manifest Destiny: The Origins of Racial Anglo-Saxonism* (Cambridge: Harvard University Press, 1981) 2.

and world dominance, was a product of the first half of the nineteenth century, the roots of these ideas stretch back at least to the sixteenth and seventeenth centuries. The Englishmen who settled in America at the beginning of the seventeenth century brought as part of their historical and religious heritage a clearly delineated religious myth of a pure English Anglo-Saxon Church, and in the seventeenth and eighteenth centuries they shared with their fellow Englishmen an elaborately developed secular myth of the free nature of Anglo-Saxon political institutions.[10]

These racial ideas took root in America as the English went about proclaiming their divine right to rule over both Native and African peoples. The Puritans, as we shall see, arrived with a view of the Indians that did not much permit for building of a multiracial society. Their vision of the new world included only people like themselves. For a while, the noble ideas of the Enlightenment kindled the hearts of many Europeans and had the moral potential of providing a philosophical foundation for building a multiracial society in America. The Enlightenment view of the human race saw all people as members of one human species capable of infinite progress. This view held sway among many European and American thinkers before 1815. It was expressed best by the philosophy of environmentalism, which argued that environment not "innate racial differences, accounted for the marked gaps in achievement between different peoples and different nations."[11] This view of humankind was so influential that it not only fired the imagination of the generation of the American Revolution but also held the hearts and minds of American intellectuals well into the early years of the nineteenth century.[12] This period was one of those crucial crossroads in the history of America where much hung in the balance, where compromise and the wrong moral choice threw America's greatest historical possibilities far off course. The ideas of the Enlightenment fell victim to the crushing and overpowering demands of the English push for racial dominance over Indians and Africans. It was a struggle, Horseman explains, "between a theoretical view of mankind and race provided by Enlightenment thought and a practical view stimulated by overt contacts between white Americans and blacks on the North American continent."[13]

We can only look back and regret what America lost as a result of building a society based upon white racial manifest destiny instead of upon multiracial justice, cooperation, and harmony. As we shall see, the former approach took America down the path of racial victimization and dehumanization of Indians and Africans and in the process poisoned the spiritual core of white America.

---

10. Horseman, 9.

11. Horseman, 98.

12. Horseman, 98.

13. Horseman, *Race and Manifest Destiny* 98.

In addition to the great historical, cultural, psychological, economic, and spiritual costs of centuries of racial oppression of these peoples, white racial manifest destiny in America delayed the achievement of world unity and peace by supporting similar racist ideas throughout the world.[14]

The First Barrier to Racial Unity: The American Indian and White Racial Manifest Destiny

Considering that in 1992 millions of people throughout the Western world will celebrate the five-hundredth anniversary of Columbus's first contact with the "New World," we should understand not only what he and other Europeans thought of the Native peoples of the Americas but also how Europeans' different cultural views of land, peoples, and religion led to the eventual subjugation of the Native American peoples. Here again, we revisit history not to belabor the role of European racial domination in the United States but to emphasize at what cost that domination took place and to note the lost possibilities of achieving racial unity and social progress. While historians might differ on the historical junctures where racial unity based upon justice and equality was possible but lost due to the expanding system of European racial dominance, they tend to agree that many of the first contacts between Europeans and Native peoples were friendly and could have developed into lasting bonds of racial unity. However, they also agree that since these relationships took place at a time when European nations were in a state of economic, political, intellectual, and religious change, it was also inevitable that the expansionist tendencies and military technological superiority of the Europeans would tip the scale towards a European racial dominance based solely on the belief that God had given them a divine right to rule over the nonwhite races of the world. When we study Columbus's first report of the first Native peoples he encountered, we cannot help but notice the characteristics he emphasized, such as the absence of iron and steel weapons:

> The people of this island and all the other islands which I have found and of which I have information, all go naked, men and women, as their mothers bore them, although some of the women cover a single place with a leaf of a plant or with a net of cotton which they make for the purpose. They have no iron or steel or weapons, nor are they fitted to use them. This is not because they are not well built and of handsome stature, but because they are very marvelously timorous. . . .It is true that, after they have been reassured and have lost this fear, they are so guileless and so generous with all they possess, that no one would believe it who has not seen it. They refuse nothing that they possess, if it be asked of them; on the contrary, they invite any one

---

14.   As we have already seen, Jefferson's writings on blacks were read throughout Europe, a fact that no doubt contributed to Europeans' negative views of African-Americans. This trend continued as white American writers on race became the leaders in the field of racist religious and quasi-scientific tracts, books, and articles throughout the nineteenth and early twentieth centuries. See Gosset, 54-122, 370-408; Wood, passim.

to share it and display as much love as if they would give their hearts. They are content with whatever trifle of whatever kind that may be given to them, whether it be of value or valueless.[15]

This idyllic view of Native peoples could not but have been attractive to certain Europeans bent on trade and conquest, events that did in fact take place not long thereafter. Columbus's report of the Native people continued in this vein:

They do not hold any creed nor are they idolators; but they all believe that power and good are in the heavens and were very firmly convinced that I, with these ships and men, came from the heavens, and in this belief they everywhere received me after they had mastered their fear. This belief is not the result of ignorance, for they are, on the contrary, of a very acute intelligence and they are men who navigate all the seas, so that it is amazing how good an account they give of everything. It is because they have never seen people clothed or ships of such a kind. . . .In all these islands, I saw no great diversity in the appearance of the people or in their manners and language. On the contrary, they all understand one another, which is a very curious thing. . . .In all these islands, it seems to me that all men are content with one woman, and to their chief or king they give as many as twenty. . . .I have not been able to learn if they hold private property; it seemed to me to be that all took a share in whatever any one had, especially of eatable things.[16]

Columbus, like most Europeans of his day, would have been interested in private property among the Native peoples, who it would be discovered had a far different view of land and the use to which it should be put than did their European visitors. Differing views of land would become the cause of some of the first conflicts between Europeans and Native peoples. Aside from these fairly positive impressions of Indians that gained popularity among educated Europeans, Columbus also created some of the first negative images of these Native peoples. While he had "found no human monstrosities," as many expected, "but on the contrary the whole population is very well formed. . .," he did claim to have come across Native peoples who

are regarded in all the islands as very fierce and who eat human flesh. They have many canoes with which they range through all the islands of India and pillage and take whatever they can. . . .They are ferocious among these other peoples who are cowardly to an excessive degree, but I make no more account of them than of the rest.[17]

---

15. Quoted in Robert F. Berkhofer, Jr., *The White Man's Indian: Images of the American Indian from Columbus to the Present* (New York: Vintage Books, 1979) 6.

16. Quoted in Berkhofer, 6.

17. Quoted in Berkhofer, 7.

Notwithstanding the former view of the loving, good-natured Natives willing to give everything they owned to outsiders, this latter view of Native people as cannibalistic, depraved, and hostile, gained as much if not at times more popularity among Europeans. More than the "good Indian" image, this "bad Indian" image provided a rationale for the later expansionist designs of those Europeans who saw America as a place that had to be rescued from the devil and saw Native peoples as barriers to be moved by God to make way for the development of a white Christian civilization. For example, Cotton Mather considered his Puritans to be "a people of God settled in those, which were once the Devil's Territories. . ." and believed that the "the Devil was exceedingly disturbed, when he perceived such a People here accomplishing the Promise of old made unto our Blessed Jesus, that '. . . He should have the Utmost parts of the Earth for his Possession. . .'."[18] The logical conclusion was clear: the Native peoples occupied unsacred land, "the Devil's Territories" that had to be claimed by the Puritans, who considered themselves to be the "Chosen People."

The Chosen-People complex of the early Puritans provided one of the first theological rationalizations for the victimization and dehumanization of the Native peoples of New England. Puritans believed that New England was an extension of their mandate that had begun in England before their migration of 1630-1642. Every barrier they overcame represented God's favor and confirmation of their spiritual destiny, even if at times God, according to their interpretation, had to destroy Native people to clear the way for his Chosen Ones. For example, the epidemic that had virtually destroyed all the Native peoples in the region just prior to the arrival of the Puritans was perceived by the Puritans as a great blessing. So firmly did early Puritans believe that this 1617 epidemic emanated from God on their behalf, that for years after the event Puritan leaders prayed thanks to God for his assistance.[19]

The same rationale prevailed in the Puritan mindset after they almost destroyed the entire Pequot tribe in 1637 and during subsequent wars against the Indian tribes in the region.[20] The Puritan's worldview made it impossible for them to coexist in a biracial society on equal terms. Many Puritans simply could not divest themselves of the rigid notion that they had a divine right to dominate the land. Puritan religious leaders and lay persons could only see their history in one way: namely, the struggle to realize their racial-religious manifest destiny. Not even the best of the "good Indians" could deter them from pursuing this vision of themselves. "Good Indians," such as Squanto, who helped the Pilgrims of the Plymouth Plantation to survive, were not seen as evidence of the potential for biracial coexistence but as God's intervention on behalf of his Chosen People, the Pilgrims. While they expected God to use the Native people as just one more instrument to help them realize their destiny,

---

18. Quoted in Wood, 228.

19. Wood, 210.

20. Wood, 210.

21. Berkhofer, 83.

they also "expected the horrors of Indian warfare both because of [their belief in] the unregenerate state of the Indians who were trapped in the 'snare of the Divell' and because God must from time to time send a scourge to chastise His chosen people in their pride and in their department from His word."[21] Such thinking could not but lead Puritans to see Native peoples as being both instruments of good and bad fortune in the unfolding destiny of a superior people. " Thus," as Berkhofer comments, "the images of the good and bad Indian served the same didactic purposes for the Puritan imagination."[22]

Even if the Puritans and other European religious denominations had been less rigid in their worldviews, encouraging instead a creative interracial coexistence between themselves and Native peoples, their other worldviews concerning the land occupied by the Natives would have remained as barriers to interracial cooperation. Many European Christians operated on the belief that they had a "right to discovery." Therefore, since native peoples were not Christians or were not divesting themselves of their Native cultures to the satisfaction of European Christians to qualify as "real Christians," then the real Christians, or Chosen People, had a right to the land. Puritans could also take possession of Native peoples' land under the European legal theory of *vacuum domicilium* by claiming that "land not 'occupied' or 'settled' went by forfeit to those who attached themselves to it in a 'civilized' manner."[23] Puritan leaders like John Winthrop applied this theory to the Native peoples even before the Puritans arrived in the New World, as Winthrop himself wrote before he landed on the shores of New England:

> As for the Natives in New England, they inclose noe Land, neither have any settled habytation, nor any tame Cattle to improve the Land by, and soe have noe other but a Natural Right to those Countries, and if we leave them sufficient for their use, we may lawfully take the rest, there being more than enough for them and us. [24]

Here again, we see the philosophical building block of the early Puritan sense of religious manifest destiny. They arrived with the arrogant assumption that they had the right to take the land of Native people whose way of life did not conform to European standards because they had "inclose[d] noe land, neither have any settled habytation, nor any tame Cattle to improve the land. . . ." The land question constituted one of the most difficult barriers to Indian-white cooperation. Few historians would deny the major role European racial and cultural arrogance played in this conflict, a conflict that still plagues Indian-white relations today.[25]

Racial unity and cooperation between Native peoples and Europeans might have had a better chance of succeeding if their two worldviews had been more

---

22. Berkhofer, 83.

23. Gary B. Nash, *Red, White, and Black: The Peoples of Early America,* 2d ed. (Englewood Cliffs, N.J.: Prentice-Hall, 1982) 79.

24. Quoted in Nash, 79-80.

25. The latest and most published Indian-white conflict over land in North America took place in Oka, Quebec, Canada, July-September, 1990.

compatible, but the weight of history proved too much. Their converging-histories based upon two vastly different worldviews were almost certainly destined to clash. However, in terms of the potential of racial unity and social progress for both European and Native peoples at the point of their initial contacts, the Native worldview was far more compatible to that end. The restless, expansionist nature of the European, coupled with an ethnocentric religious vision of Europeans as the Chosen People, simply was not compatible with any joint biracial venture in universal social progress. Far too many Europeans arrived in the New World with either a chip on their shoulders or a Bible and gun in their hands. Most did not come to join hands with the "good Indians" in building a biracial society based upon justice and social progress for all peoples, but like the Puritans to carve a white Christian civilization out of the "Devil's Territories." In many ways, the Native people offered a much more humane way of building a multiracial society. Had Columbus and his contemporaries and those who followed them been less concerned about wealth and power, they might have been able to build upon the great spiritual power of many of the Natives they first encountered. By focusing upon wealth and power and prostituting Christianity to obtain these ends, they lost great opportunities to build a multiracial society in the New World based upon genuine respect, justice, equality, and social harmony. Many of the Native people could have taught the Europeans a new way of viewing the land. Rather than regarding the land as just a resource "to be exploited for man's gain. . .[and] a commodity to be privately held" and fenced in, Europeans might have learned to see the land as a natural world that is sacred, "and inhabited by a variety of 'beings', each possessing spiritual power and all linked together to form a sacred whole."[26] To the Indian, the European notion of land being privately owned was senseless. While Native peoples did recognize territorial boundaries among tribal groups, land was held in common within these boundaries. Contrary to the European view of land as a form of commodity, Native peoples tended to view land as a part of Nature given to humans by the Creator to be used and respected. This view of land as entrusted to humans by the Creator lent a special meaning to the relationship among the people who shared the trust. As the Moravian missionary John Heckewelder discovered during his stay with the Delaware Indians in the eighteenth century, the Native view of God was that of a Creator who

> made the Earth and all that it contains for the common good of mankind; when he stocked the country that he gave them with plenty of game, it was not for the benefit of a few, but of all: Every thing was given in common to the sons of men. Whatever liveth on the land, whatsoever groweth out of the earth, and all that is in the rivers and waters. . .was given jointly to all and

---

26. Nash, 25.

27. Quoted in Nash, 26.

every one is entitled to his share. From this principle hospitality flows as from its source.[27]

Commenting on this approach, Nash says, "Thus, land was a gift of the Creator, to be used with care, and was not for the exclusive possession of particular human beings."[28] One can only imagine what kind of race relations would have evolved if Europeans had been able to accept and practice this view of the land and its relationship to people. Given that many European wars had been triggered by conflicts over land, the adoption of this Native-American approach to the Earth might have been of great benefit to the economic, social, and political stability of Europe. Most certainly, the Native view of land was less ethnocentric than that of the Puritans and generations of white Americans officials who formulated land policies that victimized and dehumanized generations of Native peoples.

Early America could also have benefitted from other aspects of Native peoples' cosmology, which no doubt would have contributed to a smoother transition to a multiracial society and universal social progress. For example, the typical European interpersonal values tended to be acquisitive, competitive, and centered around the role of the individual. These values fostered the insatiable expansionism that characterized European contacts with non-European people around the world. "Wider choices and greater opportunities for the individual to improve his status—by industriousness, valor, or even personal sacrifice leading to martyrdom—were regarded as desirable," Nash points out, "Personal ambition, in fact, played a large role in the migration of Europeans across the Atlantic in the sixteenth and seventeenth centuries."[29] However, the values of many Native peoples were just the opposite of the Europeans who colonized the New World. According to one scholar, "In contrast to the exalted position of man in Judeo-Christian tradition, the Native American cosmology conferred upon the Indian a rather humble stature." Therefore, ". . .individualism was more likely to lead to ostracism than admiration in Indian communities."[30] Once again we can only speculate how very different race relations might have been if the more universalistic values of many Native peoples had been allowed to govern at least some of the relations among the races in early American history. That this did not occur was due mainly to the persistence of European expansion and domination in the New World.

By the end of the eighteenth century, the chances for achieving a multiracial society based on equality and justice for all peoples—black, white, and red—were rapidly diminishing. Historical circumstances and the relentless greed for land and power among many European settlers in America precluded any possibility for racial justice and cooperation. The period between 1815 and

---

28. Nash, 26.

29. Nash, 26.

30. Nash, 26.

1855 witnessed a steady transformation in the collective self-image of white Americans. Examining themselves against the multiracial backdrop of their developing nation, many could only see one historical scenario: the continual expansion of white Christian civilization across America, expansion that by its nature would include the removal or extermination of the Native peoples and the continual enslavement of blacks or their removal, preferably to another country, if freed. During this period most white Americans overcame decades of moral qualms concerning the rights of Native and African peoples. They buried the high ideals of the Enlightenment and the American Revolution beneath layers of racist rationalizations and the practical power politics of the emerging white nation. Nation-building to these white Americans could only include white people. To gain credibility for both what they had already done to Native and African peoples in the past and were planning to do to them in the future, white Americans adopted an American Anglo-Saxon ideology that had the dual effect of anesthetizing them to whatever lingering moral qualms they might have had towards the victimization and dehumanization of Indians and Africans and of articulating a racial mission loud enough to drown out any audible voices still preaching justice and equality and the belief in the unity of the human race.

This racial ideology of the right of white Anglo-Saxon Americans to dominate other peoples of another color in their expansion across the continent has been explained by one scholar of racial manifest destiny: "Internally it was made quite clear that the American republic was a white Anglo-Saxon republic; other white races would be absorbed within the existing racial mass while non-white races would be rigorously excluded from any equal participation as citizens."[31] This racial ideology had a devastating impact on both Native and African peoples.

As white Americans engaged in the business of building a white nation during the period between 1815 and 1850, they found themselves in a struggle between those who still believed in the Enlightenment view of the Native "as an innately equal, improvable being" and those who believed "the Indian to be inferior, who did not wish them to be accepted as equals within American society, and who expected them ultimately to disappear." Unfortunately for the Indians, the latter view was held by those whites who were steadily gaining in political power, and whose main concern was how best to remove Indians from the path of white expansion.[32] The eighteenth-century view of the Indian as a "noble savage" was slowly fading from the public to be replaced by the image of the Indian as a tragic figure doomed to extinction by the forward motion of expansion. As more and more white settlers moved into the Mississippi Valley and into the cotton lands in the southern states, Indian lands became barriers to so-called white progress. Even those Indians who had accepted the ways of

---

31.   Horseman, 189.

32.   Horseman, 192.

white civilization by giving up certain vital aspects of their own culture (to adopt the Jeffersonian model of Indian transformation and assimilation) by becoming small farmers and owning property, could not escape the grinding wheel of white racial manifest destiny. While before 1815 and for sometime after, many whites had attacked the Indian for being unwilling or unable to accept the culture of the whites because of their "savage nature," and could point to many demoralized, scattered Indian tribes as proof of the inability of the Indians to adapt to white civilization, there were thousands of Indians in the southern states who had demonstrated their ability to adopt the ways of whites and even prosper. One would have thought that such a demonstration of Indian assimilation would have been sufficient for most whites who claimed that their anti-Indian attitudes were based upon the inability of Indians to assimilate into white society, but that was not the case. Too many whites wanted Indian land, and too many whites were willing to do whatever they had to do to get that land; assimilated Indians, like freed blacks, constituted barriers to the process of white nation-building. No matter how much they became like white Americans, they were not white.[33]

Between 1815 and 1830, the policy of Indian Removal best reflected the ideology of white racial manifest destiny as applied to the Native peoples. Not only did it represent the height of racist thinking in white-Indian relations, it also demonstrated how far many white Americans were willing to go to victimize and dehumanize Indians for the sole benefit of white avarice. It was one of the lowest points in the moral and spiritual history of white America. It involved not only moral and spiritual compromise among the white public who grew increasingly insensitive to the rights of Indians but also a twisting of the very fabric of historical truth as the general white public willingly accepted and perpetuated the racial beliefs and myths rationalizing the victimization and dehumanization of the Native peoples. It was during this period in American history, when white America was forging its racial self-image and expanding and consolidating its dominance over nonwhite peoples, that even more possibilities for building a multiracial society were lost.[34]

Indian Removal as a policy of racial manifest destiny had the strongest supporters in Tennessee, Georgia, Alabama, and Mississippi. These states led the fight in pressuring the federal government to remove the Indians from their states for no other reason than they wanted the Indians' land. It did not matter that the Indians wanted to stay. The Cherokees were the very Indians who had demonstrated the "greatest success in assimilation [and] would be the most hurt by removal westward." One of the greatest leaders, Sequoyah, exemplified the degree to which the Cherokees had assimilated and mastered the culture of whites, when he devised an alphabet for his people. The Cherokees even

33. For an example of how assimilated Indians were treated, see Horseman, 195-207; Wilcomb E. Washburn ed., *The Indian and the White Man* (Garden City, N.Y.: Doubleday & Company, 1964) 376.

34. Horseman, 190.

devised a written constitution as they put forth every effort to prove that they could adapt to white culture. But to little avail. It mattered even less to those whites who coveted their land that these were the very Indians who "had followed Jefferson's injunctions to assume white ways."[35] All that mattered was that whites in these states and their representatives wanted Indians to be removed so as to make way for whites. A long battle ensued as white political leaders on the state and national levels debated the Indian Removal policy. By the late 1820s, the southern states governments' relentless pressure on the federal government for Indian Removal caused the latter to cave in and renege on former guarantees and promises. Gradually, many friends of the southern Indians gave up from despair and frustration. As many of these "friends" abandoned the cause of the southern Indian, they began justifying their abandonment with the rhetoric of white manifest destiny: Indians were destined to become extinct before the advancement of white civilization.[36]

With the election of Andrew Jackson as president of the United States in 1828, the fate of the southern Indians was sealed. Few white leaders were as virulent in their hatred and disregard for the rights of Indians as was Jackson during his days as a soldier. While fighting against the Creeks in 1813-14, Jackson called them "savage bloodhounds and blood thirsty barbarians" and "urged his troops to exterminate them."[37] In early 1814, at the battle of Horse Shoe Bend, Jackson manifested a hatred for Indians that would stain American history for decades. After his troops had surrounded about 800 Indians, they killed almost all of them, including the women and children. After the battle, Jackson sent the cloth that had been worn by the slain Indian warriors to the ladies of Tennessee. Not satisfied with the carnage they had inflicted on the Indians, Jackson's soldiers proceeded to desecrate the dead bodies of the Indians by cutting long strips of skin from them (which they used for bridle reins) and by cutting the tips of each "dead Indian's nose to count the number of enemy bodies." [38]

The savage manner in which the Creek Indians had been treated by Jackson and his men revealed a deep current of racial disregard for the Indian people as members of the human race. The killing of Indian women and children and the deliberate desecration of the Indian dead could not but have eroded any lingering sense of a common and shared humanity between Indians and whites in the minds of Jackson and his men, and by extension, in the minds of most of the general white public who saw Jackson as a great hero. One cannot help but see in the actions of Jackson and his men, a bizarre celebration of the dehumaniza-

---

35. Washburn, 376: Horseman, 195.

36. Horseman, 200.

37. Quoted in Ronald T. Takaki, *Iron Cages: Race and Culture in Nineteenth-Century America* (Seattle: University of Washington Press, 1979) 95.

38. Takaki, 96.

tion of Indian people both living and dead that has found itself a secure place in the annals of American popular history and culture, e.g., cowboys and Indians. But even more to the point: these celebrations of offering cloth of slain Indian warriors to white women and fashioning bridle reins from strips of skin from dead Indian bodies indicated a highwater mark in the pathology of white racial hatred of nonwhites.

When Jackson was elected to the presidency in 1828, people still remembered him as the "heroic fighter." In their minds he represented their interests as whites advancing against the "red savages" standing in their way. Jackson personified the supreme architect of white racial manifest destiny at the expense of the Native peoples. After the protracted struggle between southern Indians and their white supporters and the Jackson anti-Indian forces in 1828, the federal government ordered the army to round up 15,000 Cherokees. After they were placed in detention camps, they were "marched west beyond the Mississippi in the dead of winter, more than 4,000 Cherokees died on the 'Trail of Tears'."[39] Summing up the impact of Jackson's role in the victimization and dehumanization of southern Indians, one historian writes:

> During the age of Jackson, some seventy thousand Indians were removed from their homes in the South and driven west of the Mississippi River. Due to violence, disease, starvation, dangerous travel conditions, and harsh winter weather, almost one-third of the southern Indians died. By 1844, the South was as far as Indians were concerned, a "white man's country."[40]

Jackson was not the founder of the movement of racial manifest destiny that undermined and later discarded the more racially egalitarian ideas of the Enlightenment and erected ideological barriers to the development of a multiracial society based upon justice and cooperation. However, he willingly inherited it and willingly carried it out and passed it on to posterity. For decades to come, advocates of white racial manifest destiny would continue to break treaties with Indian peoples as well as to take their land for the sole benefit of whites.[41] As late as the 1890s, a future president of the United States, Theodore Roosevelt, could still boast of the right of white people to take land from Indians and rationalized doing so: "It is nonsense to talk about our having driven most of the Indians out of their lands. They did not own the land at all in the white sense, they merely occupied it as the white buffalo hunter did. . . ."[42]

---

39. Takaki, 100.

40. Takaki, 96.

41. George Sinkler, ed., *The Racial Attitudes of American Presidents: Abraham Lincoln to Theodore Roosevelt* (Garden City, New York: Doubleday and Company, 1971) passim.

42. Quoted in Sinkler, 334.

The Second Barrier to Racial Unity: The Enslavement of Africans and the Development of White Racist Attitudes

The same white American mind-set that perceived Native peoples as barriers to the progress of white Christian civilization, that saw whites as the most important people on the continent with a racial destiny to be carried out with guns and Bibles, and that by the 1850s felt little remorse for the systematic victimization and dehumanization of the Native peoples then under way, perceived black people less as barriers to their progress and more as a form of raw material to be fashioned and used as instruments in the building of a white-only nation. Jefferson had paved the way for this view of nation-building in his *Notes of the State of Virginia.* While Jefferson did consider sharing the nation-building process with Indians,[43] by the time of Jackson, the Jeffersonian view of Indian-white cooperation in the nation-building process was fast fading from the public mind. As the process of white nation-building marginalized the Native people through conquest and removal, that same process was at work shaping black slave labor into an instrument of white economic development. The land that whites forced the Indian to abandon was all too often cultivated by black slave labor under the lash of white planters who saw both Indians and Africans as different sides of the same racial coin: their humanity could be violated without qualms for the benefit of the expanding white Christian civilization. Thus, advocates of white racial manifest destiny either could not or would not conceive of social progress emanating from racial unity; rather, they could only conceive of white social progress emanating from white racial dominance over red and black peoples.

As the dual process of conquest and removal of Indian people and the institutionalization of African slavery began, the few brave whites who visualized a country where people from all racial backgrounds could live together found themselves confronted by the behemoth of racial manifest destiny. Fewer and fewer whites were troubled by the moral contradictions of white nation-building on the stolen land of Indians and the bowed backs of African slave labor. Fewer and fewer historical windows of opportunity remained open through which white America could pass towards building a multiracial society based upon justice and cooperation. The institutionalization of African slavery as an essential component of white nation-building soon materialized as the second formidable barrier to racial unity. Once African slavery was in place legally (and in the moral comfort zone) of most of white America, the last historical windows for achieving unity vanished, not to appear again until the short experimental period of racial democracy during Reconstruction.[44]

The enslavement of the African, later rationalized by tortured logic and moral gyrations, worked a strange uneasiness into the collective psyche of

---

43.   See discussion of Jefferson in Chapter 3.

44.   Franklin and Moss, 216-23.

white America. What might have been simply another chapter in the long history of human oppression turned out to be a protracted struggle, particularly for southern whites, to define themselves in an environment peopled heavily by blacks. The social, political, cultural, and psychological ramifications of black enslavement radiated throughout white southern society and penetrated deep into the region's white collective psyche and later poisoned the soul of the nation for centuries. From the institutionalization of slavery in the mid-seventeenth century to about the 1830s, slavemasters experimented with several images of blacks to rationalize their enslavement of people whom they knew to be as human as themselves. The black sex-hungry-savage image performed one key functional need for white masters needing to subject the slave to harsh treatment, but some slavemasters liked the image of the happy slave who was loyal, dependent, and affectionate—in short, a sambo. As one slavemaster put it: "At present, we have in South Carolina, two hundred and fifty thousand civilized and peaceful slaves, happy and contente."[45] This image helped slavemasters to convince themselves that perhaps slavery was justified if only because it had transformed savage Africans into civilized, happy slaves.

These rationalizations, however, did not quiet the consciences of slavemasters. There were moral contradictions warring within the larger society that could not be easily dismissed or buried. During the period before 1830, many slavemasters admitted that slavery was plainly amoral. The American Revolutionary period held up a mirror to the slavemasters and forced them for the first time to see how blatantly hypocritical they were being in fighting for their own rights while holding others in bondage. Many, gazing in the mirror of their society, confessed that they could not justify slavery, which they knew to be "repugnant to humanity" and "destructive of liberty."[46] So troubled by this moral war waging in their collective soul were they, that not even the invention of the cotton gin and the subsequent expansion of cotton production, which infused a new life and greatly increased the profitability of black enslavement, could silence the voice of conscience among some slavemasters. They could not live with the moral contradictions related to the enslavement of black people. Slavemasters found themselves describing slavery in such terms as "an evil," "a curse," which was "felt and acknowledged by every enlightened man"[47] in the South. So persistent was this moral torment among some planters that even after the proslavery apologists had developed sophisticated arguments defending the enslavement of blacks, these slavemasters still felt the moral contradiction connected with human bondage.[48]

Despite these moral qualms, most whites clung to and rationalized slavery because of its economic benefits. For example, black slave labor was the very

45. Quoted in Takaki, 119-20.

46. Takaki, 119.

47. Takaki, 120.

48. Takaki, 120.

foundation of Thomas Jefferson's life and of his many contributions to the process of white nation-building, as a scholar of his life has pointed out so well:

> Thomas Jefferson was intimately associated with slavery from the cradle to
> the grave. His first memory was of being carried on a pillow by a slave; and
> a slave carpenter made the coffin in which he was buried at Monticello. The
> labor of black slaves made possible Jefferson's cultivation of the arts; the
> building of Monticello and the Virginia State Capitol, his principal architec-
> tural monuments; the acquisition of books which made his library one of the
> largest private libraries in the United States (and which eventually formed
> the nucleus of the Library of Congress); the accumulation of choice wines
> and the fine foods prepared by a French chef both of which made dinner at
> the President's house a notable event in the lives of congressmen; and the
> leisure which he devoted to science, philosophy, and politics. Even
> Jefferson's salaries as Secretary of State, Vice-President and President were
> indirectly paid in large part by slaves: their labor provided the tobacco,
> cotton, and sugar, the export of which stimulated Northern shipping, manu-
> facture, banking, and insurance and enabled the United States to make remit-
> tances for imported manufactured goods and to attract the foreign investment
> capital vital to the agricultural, industrial, and commercial development of
> the Republic. Next to land, slaves constituted the largest property interest in
> the country, far greater than manufacturing and shipping combined. Truly,
> one of the main pillars of world of Thomas Jefferson was black slavery.[49]

Black slave labor not only was a major pillar in Jefferson's life but also contributed substantially to the economic development of the country as well,
which might explain in part Jefferson's obsessive need to degrade and by extension to dehumanize blacks in his writings. However, he was not alone in his
attempt to resolve his moral contradictions by resorting to racial rationalizations. The black presence during the early stages of white nation-building
posed other problems besides the moral contradictions over enslaving people
chiefly for one's own economic welfare. In the process of confronting,
conquering, and enslaving peoples of color, the English found it necessary to
redefine themselves in a manner that would clarify (to themselves) their special
role in the multiracial society they were largely responsible for creating. In
fact, the process of white nation-building within the context of racial manifest
destiny involved dramatic shifts in whites' racial self-perception. Jordan
explains this shift:

> Most suggestive of all, there seems to have been something of a shift during
> the seventeenth century in the terminology which Englishmen in the colonies
> applied to themselves. From the initially most common term *Christian*, at
> mid-century there was a marked shift toward the term *English and free*.
> After about 1680, taking the colonies as a whole, a new term of self-identifi-
> cation appeared—*white*.[50]

---

49.   Miller, 1.

50.   Jordan, 52.

As whites became more conscious of their "whiteness," they became less concerned about the traditional distinctions of religion and nationality and more concerned about what they had in common. As more Africans arrived in the colonies and became assimilated into the English colonial culture joined by non-English whites, the English found themselves in a multiracial society their actions had created but that their collective minds could not begin to understand in terms of short- and long-term psychosociological effects. As both the black and the white races increased, the English, being in the dominant position in the colonies and still carrying the cultural baggage of traditional English attitudes, could not help but notice that the most profound differences were not among whites of varying religious, ethnic, and national backgrounds but between blacks and whites. "As time went on," Jordan argues, "English colonists turned increasingly to what they saw as the striking physiognomic difference. . ."[51] between the Africans and European peoples populating the colonies. In 1692, this emerging racial consciousness of whites was reflected in a revised Maryland law prohibiting miscegenation.[52] In the revised form, the term *Christian* was dropped, but the terms *white and English* were retained,[53] indicating where English colonists within an emerging multiracial society wanted the emphasis to be placed. The gradual substitution of the term *white* for *Christian* in the cultural and racial transformation of the English colonies suggests that most whites were beginning to see themselves in strictly racial terms instead of in terms of potential Christian brotherhood and sisterhood. Retaining the term *Christian* might have kept some options open to build a multiracial society based upon an appreciation of racial diversity and justice, but by this time the institution of slavery was erecting a high wall which few visionaries and advocates would be able or willing to scale to live in a just society. Being "white" had too many advantages which most whites in early English colonies could not forgo for visions of multiracial harmony.

The enslavement of Africans parallel to the development of a white nation supposedly based upon the high ideals of the Enlightenment and the American Revolution required racial rationalizations both to quiet the consciences of many whites who could not live with the moral contradictions and to educate generations of whites who were expected to carry out the mission of racial manifest destiny. A convincing system of racial rationalization was particularly crucial for the latter group because they had to be free of all moral qualms related to the conquest and removal of Indians and the enslavement of blacks if

51. Jordan, 52.

52. Jordan, 52.

53. Jordan, 52.

they were to be able to carry out their "divine" racial mission. By the mid-1660s, the English colonists were becoming accustomed to thinking of Africans more as chattel than as human beings. Already preconditioned by Elizabethan cultural images and perceptions of blackness that were further distorted by their sudden and traumatic contact with West Coast Africans and lower primates, English colonists had more than significant cultural baggage to predispose them to enslave black people and be at peace with themselves while doing so.

But other factors also contributied to the enslavement of Africans. According to Gary B. Nash, a historian of race relations in America, "Certainly a latent and still forming prejudice against people with black skin was partially responsible for the subjugation of Africans. But the chronic labor shortage in the colonies and the almost total failure to mold Indians into an agricultural labor force were probably more important factors."[54] The key point is: once the enslavement of Africans was institutionalized in early America, it "cast the Negro in such a lowly role that the initial bias against him could only be confirmed and vastly strengthened. It was hardly possible for one people to enslave another without developing strong feelings against them."[55] Mass enslavement of Africans was triggered by the initial "unfavorable impressions of Africans and economic conditions which encouraged their exploitation. . . .",[56] but much more was required to produce a racist culture and people who could oppress people with black skin without moral qualms. That "something" was the systematic institutionalization of not only African slavery but also the rationalization of white racial dominance over black people, slave or free. However, slavery was the foundation that "harden[ed] racial feelings into a deep and almost unshakable prejudice which continued to grow for centuries to come."[57] The enslavement of Africans, therefore, created the need among the vast majority of white Americans to understand their "whiteness" in relation to "the black presence" in their midst and to do so in a way that would preserve their image of themselves as moral and God-fearing people. They had to rationalize the enslavement of black human beings in order to minimize an obvious social evil. The best way to do this was by degrading the victims of their racial oppression as being unworthy of humane treatment, as not being as fully human as whites, or as being "beasts" or "children."

One of the first and most persistent rationalizations white Americans adopted to justify slavery and various other forms of racial social controls over the centuries was the idea of the insatiable sexual appetite of black people that

---

54. Gary B. Nash, "Red, White and Black: The Origins of Racism in Colonial America" in Gary B. Nash and Richard Weiss, eds., *The Great Fear: Race in the Mind of America* (New York: Holt Rinehart and Winston, 1970) 16.

55. Nash, 16.

56. Nash, 16.

57. Nash, 16.

required they be held in check. "Arising from the fear of the black slave bent upon sexual revenge," Nash explains, "was the common perception of the Negro as a hypersexual creature, another view which has transited the centuries so enduringly as to suggest that it fills a need in the white psyche."[58] Because white males dominated most aspects of early American society and culture, most white rationalizations of racial dominance of blacks on the sexual level embodied long-held sexual anxieties and fears of white males. From before Jefferson to the present, white males have used a variety of sexual myths to rationalize their domination of black people. During the colonial period, white males created a network of laws controlling sexual relations primarily between black men and white women, while at the same time exercising their right of sexual dominance over black women.[59] According to Nash, the image of blacks as hypersexual creatures intensified during the colonial period through white males' frequent sexual relations with black women. Since white males had almost complete control of blacks, they could and often did have black women whenever they so desired. But they found such sexual behavior troublesome since it reflected those same sexual urges they had attributed to their imagined hypersexual black slaves. White men who found themselves caught up in such socially contradictory behavior could extricate themselves by projecting their sexual urges and behavior onto black women. As Nash explains:

> Little evidence can be found to show that the black woman was physiologically a more sexually responsive person. Instead, the white man made her into a symbol of sexuality because he could thus act out with her all of the repressed libidinal desires which were proscribed by his own moral code, and because by assigning to her a promiscuous nature he could assuage his own guilt that festered inevitably as a result of his illicit and exploitative activities.[60]

These white-male sexual projections fed into a complex system of racial myths about blacks that rationalized white racial manifest destiny. This racial-sexual rationalization of black slavery intensified during and after black slave revolts and insurrections. White southerners "always stressed the physical threat black revolt posed for white women."[61] The Nat Turner Insurrection of

---

58. Nash, 20.

59. According to one scholar of "law and the American legal process during the Colonial Period," the colonial legal system is best understood by "recognizing that it was a system controlled by a white male-dominated culture, a society generally antagonistic toward blacks, a society wherein white males wanted to maintain their domination over both white and black females, and finally a society in which white males fervently desired to preclude any sexual relationships between black males and white females." These white male-created antimiscengenation laws were not declared unconstitutional by the United States Supreme Court until 1967. See, A. Leon Higginbotham, Jr., *In the Matter of Color: Race and the American Legal Process, The Colonial Period* (New York: Oxford University Press, 1980) 38, 42.

60. Nash, 20.

61. Joel Williamson, *A Rage for Order: Black-White Relations in the American South Since Emancipation* (New York: Oxford University Press, 1986) 28.

1831 in Virginia, which left fifty-seven whites dead and eventually led to the death of all the black insurrectionists, could not have but fueled white males' fears of black men throwing off the chains that had kept their sexual beastiality in check. When the Civil War ended slavery, the sexual fears and anxieties of many southern whites persisted. Without slavery how could blacks be controlled? By the 1890s, the image of black men in the southern white mind assumed the character of "the insatiable satyr, especially built both physically and mentally for the libidinal women they served." Such post-Emancipation sexual images of black men and women would be used by generations of whites to rationalize decades of further racial oppression of black people. Blacks became the scapegoats for those southern whites struggling to adjust to a changing social, political, and economic order.[62]

The enslavement of blacks not only enabled whites to turn blacks into instruments of their economic and political development but also forced them constantly to revise their image of blacks to fit their collective psychological needs. For example, during the Jacksonian era, blacks were not seen as barriers to white expansion as were the Indians. The millions of slaves were not to be removed from white society but were tied more firmly to white society. In short, black slaves were seen as essential to the social and economic progress of white society. The image of the black "child/savage" emerged to facilitate the rationalization of an enslavement that had burdened the consciences of many slaveholders during the Revolutionary Era. As historian Ronald T. Takaki has argued, this image of blacks had a "unique regional function" that served the needs of southern whites who needed a Sambo who was "childlike, docile, irresponsible, given to lying and stealing, lazy, affectionate, and happy."[63]

White slaveowners cherished the Sambo image because it suggested that the racist social order was correct and moral: everybody was happy, both master and slave. Planters could defend their slave society against attacks by pointing to the happy slaves being cared for by loving, caring masters who overlooked their slaves' childish behavior. But as Takaki explains, the slavemasters' "need for a Sambo was more complex than the desire to defend the peculiar institution and to mitigate guilt. The image helped to assure them that the slave was contented and controlled. Surely a happy slave would not violently protest his bondage; surely he would not slit his master's throat at night."[64]

In contrast to the savage, insurrectionist image of blacks such as Nat Turner, the Sambo image was conducive to the white planters' image of the racially unified social order where racial peace and cooperation could lead to social

---

62.   Williamson, 188, 198.

63.   Takaki, 120.

64.   Takaki, 121.

progress—as long as everybody stayed neatly in their places and did not threaten the racial social order. For decades these white views of blacks vacillated between the Sambo and the Rebel or beast/rapist according to the psychosociological needs of certain segments of the white community. By the late nineteenth century, the black image in the white collective mind ranged from seeing blacks as children to fearing them as insurrectionists or beast-rapists out to destroy white society. These two polar views characterized the South between the 1890s and about 1915. The beast-rapist view of black men tended to dominate the period. This view grew out of a new period of race relations in the South among insecure whites who no longer had the institution of slavery to set them apart from blacks. With slavery gone, their social universe lost its order. Everything was in flux, but one way of maintaining the order was by creating new forms of racial oppression to provide whites with some semblance of past racial glory. Lynching blacks became one way of maintaining racial dominance and was one of the most barbaric and sadistic forms of inhumanity in the history of Western civilization.[65] Those whites who engaged, encouraged, and observed this social ritual that included hanging, burning, amputating sexual organs and other body parts for souvenirs, represented the sociopathological depths to which racists could sink in their hatred of blacks. This pathological racial hatred even reached to the office of some southern governors, such as Cole Blease, the pro-lynching governor of South Carolina, who "received the finger of a lynched black in the mail and planted it in the gubernatorial garden."[66]

Lynching tended to be especially designed for black males, who for centuries had been at the core of the white-male dominated white culture's fears, anxieties, and fantasies concerning black people in general. Lynching and other physical forms of white racial dominance were intended to break the spirit of black males and to make them subservient. Thus, much of the history of black-white relations in the United States involved formal and informal means of controlling black males. In a white-male dominated society, dedicated for much of its history to the expansion and maintenance of white economic, political, and cultural hegemony, the control of nonwhite males, especially black males, was seen by most whites as the best way to promote social peace in a multiracial society.[67]

---

65. Williamson, 71-125; lynching blacks involved more than just hanging, which was rarely sufficient to satisfy the pathological anti-black hatred of many southern whites. Torture and dismemberment of black victims provided an outlet for these whites to vent their frustrations. As Williamson puts it so well, these whites "needed devils" (182); For a chronology of lynching, see: Ralph Ginzburg, *100 Years of Lynching* (New York: Lancer Books, 1962).

66. Wiliamson, 125.

67. Since American society has always been controlled largely by white males, who had long exhibited irrational fears and anxieties about black males, most of the formal and informal means of white racial dominance have been designed to control black males. Castration of black males was one of the most drastic forms of racial dominance use by white males. According to Jordan, this practice

The enslavement of blacks had a catalytic effect on many areas of white American life and culture as related to race. It contributed to the creation of a white culture fraught with moral and political contradictions that created a well-spring of psychosociological tensions, periodically expressed through wide swings of racial projections, physical violence, institutional constraints, pro-black rights advocacy, and genuine love and fellowship. Had science and religion been able to escape the influence of racism, they might have been able to turn the tide during the formative period of much of American racist thought after 1830. Unfortunately, the swings toward racism received strong support from religion and science.

Religion and science were used by racists throughout the formative period of American race relations to support the enslavement of blacks and were used periodically for many decades after slavery to rationalize both racial segregation and the long-term effects of racism on black behavior and attitudes.[68] The American churches failed abysmally in protecting the human rights of Indians and blacks. While many individual white Christians struggled on behalf of blacks, both slave and free, and a few Christian denominations such as the Quakers and the Mennonites opposed slavery when other denominations had long since twisted the Bible to support the enslavement of black people, most American churches in general failed to confront the ideology and beliefs of white racial manifest destiny.

As soon as the proslavery forces were able to convince the general public that slavery was good for blacks as a means of civilizing them, the rush was on to reinterpret key biblical passages to conform with and rationalize the enslavement of blacks. Just before the Civil War, the slavery issue split the white American Christian community into regional denominations, e.g., Southern

---

of white males goes back to the American colonial period and was motivated by white males' fears of black males' sexual aggression. "The white man's fears of Negro sexual aggression was equally apparent in the use of castration as a punishment in the colonies. This weapon of desperation was not employed by angry mobs in the manner which became familiar after Emancipation. Castration was dignified with specific legislative sanction as a lawful punishment in Antigua, the Carolinas, Bermuda, Virginia, Pennsylvania, and New Jersey. . . .Yet castration was not simply another of the many brands of hideous cruelty which graced the colonial criminal codes: it was reserved for Negroes and occasionally Indians. In some colonies, laws authorizing castration were worded so as to apply to all blacks whether free or slave. As a legal punishment castration was a peculiarly American experience, for there was no basis for it in English law." See, Jordan, 81; Confining black males to the most marginal forms of employment protected white males from having to compete on a fair basis with black males. See, Philip S. Foner, *Organized Labor and the Black Worker, 1617-1973* (New York: International Publishers, 1976) passim; for decades, black baseball players were not allowed to compete with white baseball players for slots in the major leagues. See, Jules Tygiel, *Baseball's Great Experiment: Jackie Robinson and his Legacy* (New York: Vintage, 1984).

68. J. Oliver Buswell, *Slavery, Segregation and Scripture* (Grand Rapids, Michigan: William B. Eardmans Company, 1964) 111. Some social scientists tended to blame the black victims of white racism for the very pathologies created by that racism. See, Daniel P. Moynihan, *The Negro Family: The Case for National Action* (Washington, D. C.: Office of Policy Planning and Research, U.S. Department of Labor, 1965).

Baptists, Northern Baptist, and the like.[69] So pervasive was the influence of racism within the white Christian community that it prompted one religious historian to comment that denomination unity among certain northern white Protestants was possible only because a "growing number of northern Protestants were willing to sacrifice Negro rights."[70] Another historian argued that if there is any consistent theme in the religious experience of Americans, "it has been that where a racial factor is present, the values of 'forgiveness, reconciliation, and love' have been largely impotent—even in church—to resolve conflict and stave off strife."[71] Still another historian commented further that racism, more than any other factor, "has undermined the credibility of Christian charity throughout American history."[72] By its refusal to use its moral forces to combat racial oppression against Indians and blacks, the white American Christian community lost its soul and the opportunity to be in the spiritual vanguard of the progressive forces supporting racial unity and justice as a means of universal social progress.

Much like religion, science, too, fell under the spell of the racism that sprang from the enslavement of blacks. Scientists on both sides of the Atlantic found themselves searching for answers to the riddle of black skin and features in contrast to those of whites. Science was soon enlisted in the debate over slavery and white supremacy, and the power of the ideas of white supremacy and black inferiority found "scientific" support in the work of many renowned and respected scientists who pioneered in the fields of ethnography, anthropology, geography, and egyptology, and who published their theories and research in some of the most respected scientific journals and books in America. Beginning in the early nineteenth century, a group of American scientists began raising questions about traditional views of human equality and the unity of the human race. They were known as "the American School," and they strongly pursued the idea that the different races of humankind were actually distinct species. The irony of this development was that many whites who believed in white racial manifest destiny, white racial supremacy, and black inferiority, could not embrace the very "scientific view" that supported their racism because it struck at the heart of their religious belief in the Creation based on one Adam and one Eve. Race scientists of the American School, however, were not deterred by the beliefs of the racists within the religious community, and they continued to pursue their interests in separate species that contributed to the racist thought of the nineteenth century.[73]

---

69. Wood, 43-73, passim; 83-111, passim.

70. Quoted in Wood, 338.

71. Quoted in Wood, 338.

72. Quoted in Wood, 338.

73. William Stanton, *The Leopard's Spots: Scientific Attitudes toward Race in America, 1815-59* (Chicago: University of Chicago Press, 1960) passim.

Enslavement of blacks, therefore, created racial myths about blacks that still prevail today in the thinking of many whites. As these racial views began serving functional psychological and social needs for whites, they found them too difficult to relinquish. The more whites came to believe that they had a special racial mission, the less they could envision building a multiracial society based upon racial justice and equality. From the colonial period to the late nineteenth century, most attempts to foster racial justice and unity failed due to the persistence of the majority of whites to build a social order for whites only. So persistent was the racism of whites that by the time of the emancipation of slaves in 1863, the vast majority of white Americans had internalized the most rampant racial beliefs about blacks. Emancipation could have provided the United States with another chance at building a new multiracial society based upon racial justice and unity, but far too many whites viewed the emancipation of blacks as a threat to their welfare. They could only see social progress in white terms. To these whites, social progress could only mean white racial dominance over peoples of color. After a short period of racial democracy during Reconstruction, white America continued to erect barriers to racial unity. By the twentieth century, the legacy of racism had taken the nation far down the path of racial hatred, conflict, and disunity.[74]

---

74. Forrest G. Wood, *Black Scare: The Racist Response to Emancipation and Reconstruction* (Berkeley: University of California Press, 1970) 17-39; C. Vann Woodward, *The Strange Career of Jim Crow* (New York: Oxford University Press, 1955).

CHAPTER 5

THE LEGACY OF WHITE RACISM
IN THE TWENTIETH CENTURY

What white Americans have never fully understood—but what the Negro can never forget—is that white society is deeply implicated in the ghetto. White institutions created it, white institutions maintain it, and white society condones it.

Report of the National Advisory Commission on Civil Disorders, 1968

The Persistence of White Racism

By the twentieth century, more than two centuries of white racial dominance over Native peoples and African-Americans had created in the minds of generations of whites the image that America was essentially a white nation moving towards its great racial destiny. The last of the great central plains Indians had been subdued and placed on reservations, and the ex-slaves and the first generation of their descendants had lived to see their greatest dreams—emancipation from slavery—realized, destroyed, replaced by newer forms of slavery and racial dominance.[1] Native peoples and the African-Americans had little to look forward to in the midst of the newer and more sophisticated forms of white racial dominance that white America was extending to other lands populated by nonwhite peoples.[2] The end of the nineteenth century had witnessed the infamous European scramble for Africa that would lead to decades of further racial oppression. In fact, peoples of color around the world, in India, Africa, China, and the "New World," shared a common oppression at the hands of whites.[3]

America was the one country that could have changed the course of the racial history of the modern world, but it missed more and more opportunities to do so. These missed opportunities represented fading lights to a watchful world

---

1. Takaki, 186-87. For the historical impact of Indian reservations on Native peoples' lives and culture, see: Vine Deloria, Jr., *God is Red* (New York: Dell Publishing Company, 1973) 17, 27-32, 218-22, 251-58; Edgar S. Cahn, ed., *Our Brother's Keeper: The Indian in White America* (Washington D.C.: New Community Press, 1969); Rayford W. Logan, *The Betrayal of the Negro* (London: Collier Books, 1969) passim; Leon F. Litwack, *Been in the Storm So Long: The Aftermath of Slavery* (New York: Vintage Press, 1980) 337-449.

2. Beginning in the early 1890s, white America leaders began extending their racial dominance to Hawaii in complete disregard for the wishes of the majority of people. They imposed a similar policy of racial dominance and expansionism on the people in the Philippines. Theodore Roosevelt was a firm believer in "the white man's burden" and justified the United States taking over the Philippines because he once said it benefitted the people. See, Rubin Frances Weston, *Racism in U.S. Imperialism: The Influence of Racial Assumptions on American Foreign Policy, 1893-1943* (Columbia, S. C.: University of South Carolina Press, 1972) 37-47.

3. Frazier, passim; Segal, vii-1.

badly in need of grand models of racial unity and fellowship. Instead of building on its heritage of democracy by extending it to all peoples, by the twentieth century white America was preoccupied with building a nation dedicated first and foremost to the social and economic well-being of whites. Notwithstanding the anti-immigrant bias of white native Americans, the most widespread and deeply felt bias was directed toward black Americans. The legacy of racism had so poisoned the soul of white America that once again America took the racial path of least resistance and embarked upon a new century of racial injustice.[4]

From the end of the Civil War to the turn of the century, the focus of American race relations shifted more and more to black/white issues in the South. The emancipation of the slaves and their subsequent shortlived political participation in regional politics placed them at the center of national attention. As a result, black/white issues came to dominate American race relations. By the turn of the century, Native peoples had been pushed to the margins of white society to such an extent that they constituted far less a threat to white Americans than did black Americans. With the pacification of the Native peoples, only blacks were left as a perennial problem for whites, and the South (where the majority of blacks lived) was expected to offer a solution. This solution turned out to be another form of white racial dominance that would victimize and dehumanize black people far into the twentieth century.

Southern Racial Segregation

This path of least resistance and compromise, what historian C. Vann Woodward has called the "Capitulation to Racism" in reference to the racial changes in the Reconstruction and Post-Reconstruction South, opened the era of racial segregation that tainted the history of American democracy for most of the twentieth century.[5] The South became a seed-bed for this newly emerging form of racial domination, and the North happily acquiesced as southern states began passing countless laws and ordinances segregating blacks from whites. "The mushroom growth of discriminatory and segregation laws during the first two decades of this century," Woodward states, "piled up a huge bulk of legislation."[6] But the trend toward racial segregation had started several decades earlier. Beginning with the 1890s, the South was rapidly influencing the nature and direction of race relations in the nation as a whole, in effect demonstrating to the North that since the majority of blacks had always lived in the South among white southerners, southerners knew what was best for blacks. No wonder southern states such as Mississippi, South Carolina, Louisiana, North Carolina could amend their constitutions so as to disenfranchise most blacks yet allow even the most unqualified whites to vote. As it had on previous occasions, the highest court in the land, the United States Supreme Court, supported the very

---

4.   Logan, 359-92; Gossett, 253-409.

5.   Woodward, 49-96.

6.   Woodward, 82.

laws that contributed the most to the racial oppression of blacks. Rayford W. Logan, one of the first scholars to study the impact of racial segregation during the Post-Reconstruction period, wrote: "Practically all the relevant decisions of the United States Supreme Court during Reconstruction and to the end of the century nullified or curtailed those rights of Negroes which the Reconstruction 'Radicals' thought they had written into laws and the Constitution."[7] During the 1870s and 1880s, the Supreme Court supported discrimination by individuals on public carriers and in public places and approved racial segregation by state action. The most infamous of the Court's decisions, Plessy v. Ferguson in 1896, saw the Court for the first time invoke "the doctrine of police powers to deny in effect the equal protection which the framers of the Fourteenth Amendment thought they had established. It was this decision by which the Supreme Court accepted the doctrine of 'separate but equal accommodations'."[8] With the sanction of the highest tribunal in the land, the South had a free hand to oppress blacks in any manner they so desired. White violence against blacks during this era of Supreme Court compliance with racial oppression was so widespread that it prompted one scholar of constitutional history and racism to comment: "This was an era in which the Supreme Court supported federal police power to regulate lotteries and oleomargarine, yet constricted the use of federal police power in incidences of racial violence."[9]

People around the world celebrated the turn of the century with expositions and congresses. Many saw a future "wherein man's aspirations for his fellows would be realized through the wonders of technology. The threshold of the century also seemed to mark a quickening in man's social awareness."[10] In America, white progressives joined in the founding of the National Association for the Advancement of Colored People (NAACP) and the National Urban League, the two major organizations that would lead the way in interracial cooperation for racial justice and the uplifting of black urban dwellers.[11] But they were mere flickers of light in a long dark tunnel of racism. Southern states, the federal government, and several presidents supported the racial status quo.[12] Maintaining their role in the vanguard of white racism, southern states continued to pass an array of laws—some almost comical in form had they not

---

7. Logan, 105.

8. Logan,105, 119; for the essential aspects of Plessy v. Ferguson, see, Derrick A. Bell, Jr., *Race, Racism and American Law* (Boston: Little, Brown and Company, 1973) 204.

9. Mary Frances Berry, *Black Resistance, White Law: A History of Constitutional Racism in America* (New York: Appleton-Century-Crofts, 1971) 126.

10. Berry, 123.

11. Nancy J. Weiss, *The National Urban League: 1910-1940* (New York: Oxford University Press, 1974); Charles Flint Kellogg, *NAACP: A History of the NAACP*, vol. 1, 1909-20 (Baltimore: Johns Hopkins Press, 1967).

12. Logan, 26-104, 347-48; Sinkler, 289-372.

been so cruel—to segregate blacks and whites in every area of life. In 1903, Arkansas ordered its state penitentiary, county jails, stockades, convict camps, "and all other places where prisoners were confined" to segregate blacks and whites. Ten years later, most southern states had similar laws. The same policy of racial segregation was applied to "the white and Negro insane, feeble minded, blind and deaf, paupers, tubercular patients, and juvenile delinquents. . . ." In 1906, Montgomery, Alabama, ordered blacks and whites to use separate streetcars. In 1915, South Carolina passed a law that prohibited textile factories from allowing their black and their white employees to work together in the same room, to use the same entrances or pay windows to receive their paychecks, or to use the same "exits, toilets, drinking-water buckets, pails, cups, dippers, or glasses at any time."[13] In 1905, it became illegal for blacks and whites to use the same park facilities at the same time. Persons who donated land for playgrounds were obligated to specify what race would use it. Blacks and whites in Atlanta, Georgia, were not permitted to visit the municipal zoo at the same time until 1940. In 1929, it was illegal for blacks and whites to use the same fishing, boating, and bathing facilities. In 1935, Arkansas went even further by segregating blacks and whites "at all race tracks and gaming establishments." Starting in 1910, several southern cities outlawed blacks and whites from living in the same areas, such as blocks and districts. These laws were declared unconstitutional in 1917. In 1915, Oklahoma ordered telephone companies "to maintain separate booths for black and white customers."[14] Florida and North Carolina even had a policy of segregating textbooks used by black students in addition to strict regulations for fumigating textbooks. In 1922, Mississippi outlawed blacks and whites from riding together in a cab unless there were more than seven passengers in the cab, and the vehicle "was traveling from one city to another." And New Orleans had an ordinance separating black and white prostitutes.[15]

Notwithstanding the regional concentration of these legal forms of white racial control, their influence spread throughout the nation. Since the vast majority of blacks lived in the South, the larger white public looked to the white South for their information about blacks. And much of what the white South said and wrote about the black South became "facts" in the minds of generations of white Americans outside the region. Northern and southern whites who supported racial segregation in the South had to defend it, and the best way to defend racial segregation was to follow the examples of the pro-slavery-apologists and racial theorists who placed the blame of slavery on the backs of black slaves. Between 1900 and 1930, the defenders of racial segregation in the South produced a range of anti-black literature. I.A. Newby, a scholar who

---

13.   John Hope Franklin, "History of Racial Segregation in the South," *Annals of the American Academy of Political and Social Science* 34 (March 1956): 8.

14.   Franklin, 8.

15.   Franklin, 6-8.

studied anti-black thought among white Americans during this period, points out that, "these were the years in which anti-Negro thought reached its zenith, the years which produced the greatest proliferation of anti-Negro literature, and the years in which that literature enjoyed its broadest appeal."[16] Much like their nineteenth-century counterparts, twentieth-century racists clothed their racial theories and beliefs in scientific rationales. "The science of race which developed in this country in the early twentieth century," Newby argues, "was all inclusive, especially as it applied to the Negro. It commenced by affirming that his inferiority began with the racial differentiation of mankind, and it concluded with scientific justification for Southern race policies and prejudices."[17]

Racial segregation in the South received its greatest support from the churches. Armed with many of the proslavery religious arguments, twentieth-century religious racists continued to pervert Christianity and the Bible to support white racial dominance. Unlike the community of scientists and scholars, most white churches clung to their racist beliefs long after such beliefs were losing favor in other areas of American society. As Newby once again explains:

> . . .organized religious bodies still endorsed or failed to condemn racist policies. Long after scientists and scholars had dropped their belief in racial inequality, anti-Negro ideas endured among many American church groups. Especially true of fundamental churches in the South, this fact indicated the peculiar way in which American churches reflect popular opinion."[18]

Racism and Racial Conflict in the Industrial North

Although the South led the way in expanding and perfecting institutional mechanisms of white racial dominance of blacks, the North played a complementary role by not only adopting a "hands-off policy" but also by supporting southern racial practices in words and deeds.[19] The North, however, soon found itself facing its own variety of racism and racial conflicts when World War I triggered a need for southern black labor to replace thousands of European immigrants returning to their homelands to fight in the war. Almost overnight northern industrial centers found themselves inundated with tens of thousands of southern black "peasants" eager to work in the high-wage factories. In the space of a few years, northern cities with only a few blacks before the war had thousands in their postwar populations. The migration of southern blacks into northern cities radically changed the nature of race relations in America. No longer was the South the center of the nation's racial problems.[20]

---

16. I.A. Newby, *Jim Crow's Defense: Anti-Negro Thought in America, 1900-1930* (Baton Rouge: Lousiana State University Press, 1965) xi.

17. Newby, 21.

18. Newby, 85.

19. Logan, 165-241.

The war and the northern demand for cheap, abundant black labor changed all that. Now, the North had to share in carrying the burden of the country's most persistent social problem.

Northern cities soon discovered that they had a serious racial problem. In their haste to meet the demand for war production, many industrialists imported southern black workers to break the strikes of white workers. This soured relations between blacks and whites for decades and led to several serious race riots in the North, the worst being the Chicago race riot of 1919.[21] As more southern blacks left the South to work and live in the North, they began clashing with whites over housing. Largely because of racially restrictive convenants that were not declared constitutionally unenforceable until 1948,[22] blacks were increasingly forced to live in the worst areas of the cities.

By the 1920s, black ghettoes, infested with crime and violence, had become the norm in many northern black areas. Similar to their conterparts in the South, many northern white city officials erected barriers to control the population movement of northern blacks. These officials were supported by white citizens who organized countless white neighborhood associations to prevent blacks from moving into white neighborhoods. Throughout the 1930s and 1940s, many northern whites resorted to violence to keep blacks from-purchasing homes in "their" neighborhood.[23]

These whites were encouraged to practice such racism against blacks seeking decent housing by an agency of the federal government, the Federal Housing Administration, which encouraged and supported racially restrictive covenants. The result of such government-supported, institutionalized racism was increased racial conflict between blacks whose housing needs were not being met and those whites who believed that their property values would decrease if blacks moved into their neighborhoods. In Detroit, during the summer of 1942, racial conflicts over housing exploded into a race riot. By the next summer, another race riot, linked to a combination of racial conflicts over jobs and housing, shocked the nation. It was the worst race riot in American history.[24]

---

20. Charles Johnson, "Substitution of Negro for European Immigrant Labor" in *National Conference of Social Work Proceedings* (May-June, 1926) 319-20; Harold M. Baron, *The Demand for Black Labor: Historical Notes on the Political Economy of Racism* (Cambridge, Mass: Radical America, 1971) 19-21; Emmett J. Scott, *Negro Migration during the War* (New York: Arno Press, 1969) 26; Florette Henri, *Black Migration North, 1900-1920* (New York: Doubleday, 1926) 49-80.

21. William M. Tuttle, Jr., *Race Riot: Chicago in the Red Summer of 1919* (New York: Atheneum, 1972) 105-56.

22. Clement E. Vose, *Caucasians Only: The Supreme Court, The NAACP and the Restrictive Covenant Cases* (Berkeley and Los Angeles: University of California Press, 1967) 1-12, 12, 177-210.

23. See chapter on "Life and Death in the Inner City," Henri, 93-131; For examples of whites using bombs to force blacks out of white neighborhoods, see Tuttle, 157-83; Karl E. Taeuber and Alma F. Taeuber, *Negroes in Cities: Residential Segregation and Neighborhood Changes* (New York: Atheneum, 1972) 43-55.

Racial tension and conflict in northern cities were almost always associated with institutionalized racism. Racial discrimination in housing and employment clashed with the increased expectations of those southern blacks who had migrated North not only to get better paying jobs in northern factories but also to escape the racially repressive atmosphere of the South. Once in the North, many refused to accept even the more moderate forms of white racism. The generation that grew to maturity in the North became known as the "The New Negro."[25] Much more radical and self-assured than their parents could afford to be in the South, this new generation of blacks demanded equal treatment from whites. When such treatment was not given, they formed powerful protest groups and fought for their rights. During the 1930s, this generation of northern blacks was able to use their increased population base to exercise their political muscle in city, state, and, particularly, in national presidential elections. When World War II broke out, this generation of blacks refused to defer their agenda for the sake of the war. Led by such leaders as A. Philip Randoph of the Brotherhood of Sleeping Car Porters, they threatened a march on Washington, D.C. if President Roosevelt did not take action against discrimination in war industries. He responded with an executive order against racial discrimination in war-production industries, but white racism persisted.[26]

In some ways World War II resembled World War I in the impact that it had on American race relations. Both wars triggered black migration to northern cities and increased racial tensions and conflicts because of the unwillingness of whites to alter the racial status quo. However, the political empowerment of blacks in northern cities during the 1930s and early 1940s provided them with leverage to challenge and alter some aspects of institutional racism. In addition, northern blacks entered into several very effective interracial coalitions with progressive whites in labor and politics, coalitions that greatly augmented their struggle against racism. For example, the movement of industrial unionism led by the Congress of Industrial Organizations (CIO) supported racial equality on the job and supported black workers in their fight against racial discrimination in housing.[27]

World War II also aroused white fears and anxieties concerning the increase and expansion of the black population. The racial status quo was under attack everywhere, particularly since the war was seen by many in part as a struggle

---

24. Taeuber and Taeuber, 20; Vose, 225-27; Dominic J. Capeci Jr., *Race Relations in Wartime Detroit: The Sojourner Truth Housing Controversy of 1942* (Philadelphia: Temple University Press, 1984); Robert Shogan and Tom Craig, *The Detroit Race Riot: A Study in Violence* (Philadelphia and New York: Chilton Books, 1964).

25. Alain Locke, *The New Negro* (New York: Albert & Charles Boni, 1925).

26. Florence Murray, ed., "National Defense Chronology for the Year, 1941," *The Negro Handbook* (New York: Wendell Mailliet and Company, 1942) 76-77; Louis Ruchames, *Race, Jobs and Politics: The Story of FEPC* (New York: Columbia University Press, 1953) 20-21.

27. *CIO News*, June 28-August 21, 1943.

against the racist theories of Hitler's Germany. Roosevelt's executive order against racial discrimination, the first of its kind in history, constituted in the minds of many whites a challenge to their racial privileges. This was the period when the labor market was characterized by what some labor market scholars now called a dual labor market, which segregated black and white workers on the basis on color instead of skills.[28] Generations of whites have in many cases gained benefits over blacks on the basis of their color instead of their skills. No matter what levels of skills black workers had, the vast majority were forced to work in the most dangerous and dirtiest jobs—those jobs rejected by whites. For years many labor organizations, such as the railroad brotherhoods and the American Federation of Labor (AF of L), supported such white racial privileges. As efforts mounted against such racist practices and traditions in the labor market, white workers in various industries throughout the country responded with "hate-strikes," so-called because their only objective was to preserve the racial privileges of those white workers who refused to work alongside black workers.[29]

Perhaps the worst case of government-sponsored racism during the war involved the relocation and internment of thousands of West Coast Japanese-Americans to concentration camps in other states. Due to the anti-Japanese hysteria that resulted from the Japanese bombing of Pearl Harbor, the United States government forced entire Japanese-American communities to leave their friends and property. Forced by a deadline to leave by an appointed date, many Japanese-Americans had no choice but to sell their homes and businesses at a great loss. Many of these people had been born in the United States. But a long history of anti-Asian racism on the West Coast and the bombing of Pearl Harbor combined in a groundswell of fear and hatred that forced their removal and internment. No other American ethnic group whose native country was at war with the United States ever suffered such humiliation and shame. It was inconceivable to most white Americans to consider such treatment for German-Americans. Notwithstanding this humiliation and shame, Japanese-Americans served with distinction in the United States Armed Services.[30]

The increased racism and racial conflicts generated by the war forced some white leaders to reflect more seriously on the long-term effects of racial discrimination. Until World War II and the full revelations of the genocide against European Jews and other so-called non-Aryan peoples, far too many observers

---

28.   David M. Gordon, *Theories of Poverty and Underemployment, Orthodox, Radical and Dual Labor Market Perspectives* (Lexington, Mass: D. C. Heath and Company, 1972) 43-52; For an example of how a dual labor market affects black workers, see Harold M. Baron and Bennett Hymer, "The Negro Worker in the Chicago Labor Market," Julius Jacobson, ed., *The Negro and America Labor Movement* (Garden City: Anchor Books, 1968) 232-85.

29.   Philip S. Foner, *Organized Labor and the Black Worker, 1619-1973* (New York: International Publishers, 1976) 265-66, 280.

30.   Bill Hosokawa, *Nisei: The Quiet Americans* (New York: William Morrow and Company, 1969) 224-378, 393-422.

and scholars of race relations did not realize the extent to which the racism created by Europeans centuries ago could grow into such a monster. As long as the victims of American and European racism belonged to the non-white races, most whites either showed little concern or considered it a problem that society could take its time solving. The prevailing view was that racism would fade away in due course as whites became more enlightened and nonwhites became more civilized. However, Germany changed that thinking for many American whites who, had they been in Germany during the Third Reich, might not have been Aryan enough for its racial theorists.

The racial theories of the Third Reich emanated in part from centuries of European racist thought that had victimized and dehumanized nonwhites around the world. European Jews were among the first large-scale "white" victims of practices based on those theories. The Nazis, therefore, did not invent any startlingly new racial theories to justify their special brand of European racism. As George L. Mosse, in his groundbreaking book on the history of European racism has explained: "The Nazis did not invent racism; they merely activated it. . . .The Nazi implementation of racial policy was essentially the climax of a long development. . .from its source in the eighteenth century. The streams flows on into the future."[31]

Unfortunately, the racial lessons of the Jewish holocaust as related to the racial discrimination against blacks in the United States were lost on many white Americans during the post-war period, and the connections between blacks and Jews as victims of the same stream of European racism is often ignored in current discussion of the holocaust. "Historically, Jews and blacks have always played the outsider, the villain who threatens the tribe. Who knows," Mosse points out, "that 6 million Jews might not have been joined by as many blacks had these lived in the midst of the people of Europe."[32] Writing in 1978, Mosse reminds the reader that

> the holocaust has passed. . . .But racism itself has survived. As many peo-
> ple as ever before think in racial categories. There is nothing provisional
> about the lasting world of stereotypes. That is the legacy of racism every-
> where. And if, under the shock of the holocaust, the postwar world
> proclaimed a temporary moratorium on anti-Semitism, the blacks on the
> whole remained locked into a racial posture which never varied much from
> the eighteenth century to our time. . . .Nations which had fought against
> National Socialism [in Nazi Germany] continued to accept black racial
> inferiority for many years after the war, and did not seem to realize that all
> racism, whether aimed at blacks or Jews, was cut of the same cloth.[33]

---

31. George L. Mosse, *Toward the Final Solution: A History of European Racism* (New York: Harper & Row, 1978) 231.

32. Mosse, xi.

33. Mosse, 235-36.

After World War II, race riots and hate strikes in major northern industrial cities followed on the heels of new waves of southern black migrants eager to find work and new homes. The war years brought even larger numbers of southern blacks to northern cities where, unfortunately, even when they could find jobs, they could not find decent housing. Throughout the war and the early years of the post-war period, blacks could only find housing in traditionally black areas. As the ghettoes swelled to capacity, spawning crime and violence, black leaders, led by the NAACP, began chipping away at the various legal mechanisms used to keep the expanding black population locked in ghettoes. The vast majority of whites were determined to keep blacks from leaving the ghettoes. They had powerful white-dominated institutions, government agencies, and professional organizations to assist them. Even after the 1948 Supreme Court decision declared racially restrictive convenants unenforceable, local white real estate boards, still acting under the powerful influence of the National Association of Real Estate Boards, penalized white real estate salespersons for selling property in white areas to blacks.[34] The nature of this resistance to legal changes in the racial status quo proved revealing, as one scholar of the period explained:

> The Supreme Court decision in the 1948 cases did not change the minds of most [white] real-estate salesmen. That decision made their position of greater importance for they could enforce segregation whereas the Court could not.[35]

The manner in which the white real estate establishment went about circumventing the spirit of the law of the highest tribunal in the land demonstrated the extent to which many whites would go to maintain their racial privileges. One method they used was the following:

> The method now being used here. . .is to have the Real Estate Exchange zone the city and forbid any member of the exchange under pain of expulsion to sell property in the white zone to a Negro. If the real estate men refused to participate in the sale, the breaches will at least be minimized to those who deal with each other directly or through a. . .non-member who could be easily identified and boycotted more or less by all the people to whom the knowledge comes.[36]

Such methods kept thousands of blacks from exercising their rights to buy decent homes in which to raise families and contribute to the larger society. For

---

34.   Vose, 224-25.

35.   Vose, 223.

36.   Vose, 223.

decades, these and other methods, such as red-lining[37] by banks, forced blacks who could afford to purchase homes to live in increasingly crowded ghettoes. The whites who designed and supported these racist methods contributed to the web of urban institutionalized racism that created and maintained black ghettoes. Several decades later, after the black urban rebellions of the 1960s, the Kerner Commission Report correctly placed the blame squarely on institutionalized racism for the creation of the black ghettoes: "What white Americans have never fully understood—but what the Negro can never forget—is that white society is deeply implicated in the ghetto. White institutions created it, white institutions maintain it, and white society condones it."[38]

During the 1940s and 1950s, race relations between blacks and whites underwent dramatic and complex changes due largely to the convergence of economic, political, social, and technological changes within the larger society. New highway construction opened the suburbs to young, white, middle-class families anxious to leave the crowded city with its expanding black populations. Innercity factories and related businesses soon followed. Technological changes and the need to compete forced many industries that had once depended heavily upon several generations of unskilled southern black workers to rely more on technology instead of black brawn. As these industries became less labor intensive and more capital intensive, they hired fewer and fewer unskilled black workers. Many of these black workers would have been able to find employment in the suburbs *if* they could have found places to live, but the vast majority of whites were determined to keep blacks out.[39]

Further complicating the situation in northern cities was the emerging mechanization of southern agriculture that was beginning to replace thousands of black farms workers with tractors. Tens of thousands of these displaced rural workers, among the poorest and most uneducated in the country due to decades of racial exploitation of entire families, flooded into northern cities. But, unlike earlier southern black migrants whose lack of skills and formal education matched the demand for their labor, these displaced rural workers arrived during a period when such demand was rapidly declining. These latest black

37. "Historically the word 'redlining' originated with the alleged practice of some mortgage lenders using a red crayon to define on a map the boundaries of some areas within which they would not lend." This is the practice 'of rejecting a loan applicant on the basis of an initial characteristic of the borrower such as color or sex." Jack M. Guttentag and Susan M. Wachter, *Redlining and Public Policy* (New York: New York University Graduate School of Business Administration, Monograph Series in Finance and Economics, 1980) 11.

38. *Report of the National Advisory Commission on Civil Disorders* (New York: Bantam Books, 1968) 2.

39. *Report*, 251-60; Mark L. Gelfand, *A Nation of Cities: The Federal Government and Urban America, 1933-1965* (New York: Oxford University Press, 1975) 222-35; Joe T. Darden, Richard Child Hill, June Thomas, and Richard Thomas, *Detroit: Race and Uneven Development* (Philadelphia: Temple University Press, 1987) 15-23, 137; Arnold R. Hirsch, *Making the Second Ghetto: Race & Housing in Chicago, 1940-1960* (Cambridge: Cambridge University Press, 1983) 69-95.

migrants—many poor, uneducated, and desperate—contributed to the ever-expanding black ghettoes, now teeming with even more poverty, unemployment, underemployment, crime, and violence, and characterized by an increasing resentment and hatred of the surrounding white society many blacks knew to be at least partially responsible for maintaining their sordid conditions.[40] As the black ghettoes grew more menacing to white city officials and the surrounding white communities, whites began to rely more on institutionalized methods to check and control what they believed to be a threat to the social order.[41] The stage was set for the black urban explosions of the 1960s.

Changes in the Racial Status Quo: Challenges, Compromises, Resistance, and Denial

Even while institutionalized racism kept the vast majority of blacks locked in ghettoes with their terrible schools, confined black workers to the worst jobs, and in the South denied blacks both the right to vote and equal access to public accommodations, among other indignities, these forms of racism did not go unchallenged. From the late 1940s to the mid-1960s, every form and expression of historic white racism was challenged, and many were overcome. In 1947, Jackie Robinson broke the color barrier in major league baseball that "shook American society as profoundly as the Supreme Court's decision to desegregate education a few years later."[42] In 1948, the Supreme Court declared racially restrictive convenants constitutionally unenforceable. That same year President Truman issued his Executive Order 9981 desegregating the United States Armed Forces, a major historic step in challenging one of the bulwarks of institutionalized racism.[43]

Largely as the result of the sustained and uncompromising struggles of black organizations and their white allies, as well as the changing international climate that forced American leaders to demonstrate to an increasingly watchful world that America was doing its best to eliminate racial discrimination against

---

40.   Harry Dillingham and David Sly, "Mechanical Cotton Picker and Negro Migration." *Human Organization* 25 (Winter,1966): 344-51; William Julius Wilson, *The Truly Disadvantaged: The Inner City, the Underclass and Public Policy* (Chicago: University of Chicago Press, 1987) 34; Kenneth B. Clark, *Dark Ghetto: Dilemmas of Social Power* (New York: Harper and Row, 1965) 81-111; Report 2, 274.

41.   For decades predominantly white police forces performed the institutionalized function of maintaining control over urban black populations. See, "The Police and the Community," in Report 299-310; David H. Bayley and Harold Mendelsohn, *Minorities and the Police: Confrontation in America* (Toronto: The Free Press, 1969) 109-92; Homer Hawkins and Richard Thomas, "White Policing of Black Populations: A History of Race and Social Control in America," in Cashmore and E. Mclaughlin, eds., *Police and Ethnic Minorities in America* (London: Routledge, forthcoming 1991).

42.   Tygiel, backcover.

43.   Gerald David Jaynes and Robin M. Williams, Jr., eds., *A Common Destiny: Blacks in American Society* (Washington, D.C.: National Academy Press, 1989) 64.

its largest minority,[44] a steady stream of presidential, congressional, and judicial decisions, orders, and legislation "aimed at dismantling barriers to black participation appeared."[45]   Among these were the following: The 1954 Supreme Court Decision in Brown v. Board of Education of Topeka, which ruled against segregating blacks and whites in public schools; President Eisenhower's 1955 Executive Order 1059, which set up the President's Committee on Government Employment Policy to fight discrimination in employment. This committee replaced the Fair Employment Committee established by President Truman in 1948. In 1955, the Interstate Commerce Commission issued an order banning segregation of passengers on trains and buses in interstate travel; two years later, the 1957 Civil Rights Act created a six-member presidential commission to investigate allegations of the denial of citizens' voting rights. In 1960, another Civil Rights Act was passed to strengthen the investigatory powers of the 1957 Civil Rights Commission. In 1961, President Kennedy established the Committee on Equal Employment Opportunity to combat discrimination in employment. That same year, the Justice Department moved against discrimination in airport facilities under the provisions of the Federal Airport Act and against discrimination in bus terminals under the Interstate Commerce Commission Act. A year later, President Kennedy issued Executive Order 11063 barring discrimination in public housing receiving federal funds. In 1964, the Civil Rights Act banned discrimination in public accommodations and employment. In 1965, the Voting Rights Act suspended literacy tests and sent federal examiners into many localities to protect the rights of black voters. And in 1968, fair housing legislation prohibited discrimination in the sale or rental of housing.[46]

One has to wonder why over two decades of presidential executive orders, congressional and judicial decisions and orders, involving so much energy and time, were necessary just to insure that black Americans had the same rights as white Americans. Why at that stage of American history was it so difficult for many whites to see their fellow black citizens as equal? White Americans did not need such governmental efforts on their behalf to exercise their basic rights, but far too many white Americans at the time (and even many at the present

---

44. Black involvement in the United Nations and black organizations' petitions to the U.N. criticizing American racism (e.g., National Negro Congress in 1946, NAACP in 1947) forced white American leaders and government officials and leaders to acknowledge the damaging effects of American racism on the nation's image as a model democracy for the world to emulate. Racial discrimination and violence against black American citizens forced the State Department's "Voice of America" to include in its first broadcast to Communist Russia a report on a lynching of a young southern black being held on suspicion of murder. See, Roy Wilkins with Tom Mathews, *The Autobiography of Roy Wilkins: Standing Fast* (New York: Penguin Books, 1984) 198; John Hope Franklin and Alfred A. Moss, Jr., *From Slavery to Freedom: A History of Negro Americans,* 6th ed.(New York: Alfred A. Knopf, 1988) 408-510.

45. Jaynes and Williams, 64.

46. Jaynes and Williams, 65.

time) could not abandon their sense of white superiority. Sadly, all these efforts fell short in one way or another because of white resistance.

As we have seen, beginning with Roosevelt's executive order against discrimination in employment and notwithstanding the endorsement of his high office, many whites refused to relinquish their traditional racial privileges. Many whites on every social level resisted changes in the racial status quo. No less a famous American than President Dwight Eisenhower, in office at the time of the 1954 Supreme Court Decision, the most monumental judicial decision affecting basic human rights in American society in over a half-century, and a man who became famous as one of the greatest generals in the Second World War, fighting against one of the worst violators of human rights in modern history, no less a man, refused to support the decision. "No help would come from the White House," Harvard Sitkof, a leading scholar in the field of modern American race relations stated. "The President of the United States. . .declined to join the battle against segregation. He refused to endorse or support the Brown ruling."[47] Not only did he not endorse or support the Brown decision but President Eisenhower also often remarked: "I don't believe you can change the hearts of men with laws or decisions." He was so upset with the decision that he told one of his aides:

> I am convinced that the Supreme Court decision set back progress for in the South at least fifteen years. . . .It's all very well to talk about school integration—if you remember you may also be talking about social disintegration. Feelings are deep on this. . . .And the fellow who tries to tell me you can do these things by force is just plain nuts.[48]

Eisenhower would have preferred education over what he perceived to be unreasonable force, but as Sitkof pointed out, the president "would not educate." Instead, President Eisenhower "rejected all pleas that he tour the South seeking compliance of southern moderates, or appeal on television to the nation for understanding. He simply did not favor school desegregation, much as he had never approved desegregation of the armed forces. . . ."[49] Furthermore, he regretted appointing Earl Warren (the Chief Justice who rallied support among the justices for the 1954 decision to be unanimous) to the Supreme Court, as the "biggest damm mistake I had ever made."[50] Chief Justice Warren also had his own regrets. In his memoirs, Warren expressed disappointment in President Eisenhower's lack of support for the Brown decision, going so far as to suggest that if the president had placed the weight of his great popular appeal

47. Harvard Sitkof, *The Struggle for Black Equality, 1954-1980* (New York: Hill and Wang, 1981) 26.

48. Sitkof, 25.

49. Sitkof, 25.

50. Sitkof, 25.

on the side of the Brown decision "we would have been relieved, in my opinion, of many of the racial problems which have continued to plague us."[51]   But President Eisenhower was more concerned about the white South than about the long history of segregated education in the South that had underdeveloped generations of black children.   Instead, he told the chief justice that white southerners "are not bad people.   All they are concerned about is to see that their sweet little girls are not required to sit in school alongside some big overgrown Negro."[52]   In that statement alone, President Eisenhower, almost two centuries removed from the time of Jefferson, echoed the latter's (and many white males') greatest and most persistent fear of what might result from any challenge to the racial status quo.

Had he chosen to do so at the time, President Eisenhower could have paved the way for racial justice, equality, and racial unity, which, in turn, would have saved the country much time and energy spent on addressing the racial conflicts in the South during the Civil Rights Movement.   Instead, he chose not to endorse a vision of a more racially equal America.   His choice to back away from clear racial justice no doubt sent a clear message to many white Americans that it was alright to resist the decision of the Supreme Court to desegregate.   Since he had already gone on record in opposition to the desegregation of the armed services, President Eisenhower's words and deeds could not but have legitimized an era of white resistance to racial equality, racial unity, and social progress.   Several years later, during the Fall of 1957, this trend of white resistance came back to haunt him.   Governor Orval Faubus of Arkansas defied a federal court's order to desegregate Central High School in Little Rock.   White mobs rushed to the city to prevent nine black youths from integrating the school.   The scene of thousands of whites milling around a few black kids, who were also prevented from entering the school by the National Guard, attracted worldwide attention.   President Eisenhower was forced to assume leadership in this racial crisis.   He sent federal troops to the city to "uphold national supremacy, defend presidential authority, enforce the law of the land.   In so doing, Eisenhower became the first president since Reconstruction to use armed troops in support of Negro rights."[53]

While the Warren Court did pave the way through its historic, landmark decision, it adopted a gradualist policy of the implementation of its decision that lasted more than a decade.   It took a mass movement, the Civil Rights Movement, finally to overcome some of the gradualist tendencies of the three branches of government.[54]

---

51.   J. Harvie Wilkinson, III, *From Brown to Bakke: The Supreme Court and School Integration 1954-1978* (New York: Oxford University Press, 1979) 24.

52.   Wilkinson, 24.

53.   Sitkof, 32-33, 41-198.

54.   Wilkinson, 131-249: Gary Orfield, *Must We Bus? Segregated Schools and National Policy* (Washington, D.C.: The Brookings Institution, 1978) passim.

The Civil Rights Movement triggered a groundswell of white violence, murder, and intimidation in the South. But in the process, the movement also generated one of the most impressive displays of interracial unity and fellowship that the modern world had ever witnessed. Unfortunately, when the struggle against institutionalized racism and its effects moved to the North, a new kind of white resistance surfaced. Many northern whites tended to support desegregation in the South but shied away from desegregation in the North. With the onset of bussing as a means of school integration in the North, particularly during the 1970s, northern whites began to realize their payments on historic racism were finally due. Bussing children to achieve racial integration became the most explosive issue of the 1970s and led to much confusion, pain, and anguish among blacks and whites alike.[55] Like southern white resistance to changes in the racial status quo, northern white resistance was no less racist in nature and purpose; most were primarily concerned with maintaining a racial comfort zone in which they could dictate the nature and pace of racial changes.

Starting with the white backlash of the late 1960s that continued into the 1970s, many whites began to grow weary of the protracted struggle over racism. Other issues began competing with racial issues. The black urban rebellions had frightened many whites who then fled to the suburbs and turned their backs on the problems of the increasingly black central cities. A tendency emerged among many of these whites to blame increasing black poverty, crime, and violence on blacks themselves. This "blaming the victim"[56] syndrome provided an emotionally comforting escape for many whites who wanted to disassociate themselves from the historic burden of racism.[57] Much like the historic pattern of white collective guilt over slavery among some planters—guilt that was dissipated by pro-slavery apologists who shifted the blame of slavery onto the slaves themselves—from the 1970s to the present time, many whites began taking on a form of collective denial of the legacy of racism. With the advent of affirmative-action policies and programs to address the lingering effects of institutionalized racism, these whites and their apologists have postulated a theory of reverse discrimination[58] that has gained credence in many respectable circles. It goes without saying that these developments do not bode well for racial unity.

-----

55. Sitkof, 220-23. Several studies on white racial attitudes and the "white backlash" are still a bit contradictory. See, Jaynes and Williams, 120-21.

56. William W. Ryan, *Blaming the Victim* (New York: Random House, 1971).

57. Jaynes and Williams, 150; Norman C. Amaker, *Civil Rights and the Reagan Administration* (Washington, D. C: The Urban Institute Press, 1988) 115-30; Nathan Glazer, *Affirmative Discrimination: Ethnic Inequality and Public Policy* (New York: Basic Books, 1975) 77-222; Nijole V. Beneokraitis and Joe R. Feagin, *Affirmative Action and Equality: Action, Inaction, Reaction* (Boulder: Westview Press, 1978) 171-86.

58. One widespread criticism of affirmative action is that it has resulted in "reverse-discrimination"—that is, in hiring and promoting women and minorities over presumably better qualified white males. See Beneokraitis and Feagin, 84.

Black Awareness, Urban Rebellions, Political Empowerment, and Separation

White resistance, compromise, and denial had a devastating effect on black people and greatly complicated efforts at achieving a racially integrated society. Many blacks resented white resistance to their legitimate claims for racial justice and equality. The protracted delays of the Supreme Court and the lack of support from many white leaders eroded the trust of young blacks who had been taught to believe in racial integration. These young blacks, especially black college students, began questioning the value of racial integration, shifting their attention to emerging black nationalistic movements that emphasized black cultural values and separation from whites. The icons of the Civil Rights Movement, such as Martin Luther King, James Farmer, Thurgood Marshall, and others who had fought racial segregation for decades, began losing their influence among these young black radicals. No longer were these young people interested in integrating into what they considered to be a corrupt white society. New cultural heroes began emerging—Malcolm X, Huey Newton, LeRoi Jones, Stokely Carmichael, Rapp Brown, among others. These new heros did not share the values of the traditional civil rights establishment. As the last days of the Civil Rights Movement began to fade in the rising heat of the anti-war movement and the white backlash of the late 1960s and early 1970s, blacks had already entered what historian Alton Hornsby characterized as "an age of disillusionment."[59] The sad irony of this "age of disillusionment," the years between 1964 and 1973, was that 1964 witnessed not only the beginning of black urban rebellions but also the awarding of the Nobel Peace Prize to Martin Luther King, Jr., "the champion of non-violent resistance to racial oppression."[60]

Throughout the 1960s, black urban rebellions in the North and South shook the nation to its core. The Civil Rights Movement had no answers or solution for this phase of the legacy of racism. While the movement itself had led the way in overcoming legal barriers to racial equality and had won impressive victories for blacks in integrating southern public schools and public accommodations and, most important, in securing passage of the 1965 Voting Rights Act that opened the way for the most significant political empowerment of southern blacks in history, it could not address the complex social and structural problems affecting the majority of poor and desperate blacks festering in the declining central cities of the North and South. Historic racism combined

---

59. Benjamin Muse, *The American Negro Revolution: From Nonviolence to Black Power* (New York: Citadel Press, 1970) 230-50, 299; Sitkof, 167-91; Franklin and Moss, 458-67; Alton Hornsby, Jr., *The Black Almanac: From Involuntary Servitude (1619-1860) to a Return to the Mainstream?* (New York: Barron's Educational Series, 1977) 120-227.

60. Hornsby, 120.

with structural changes in the urban economy had created a desperate situation for these blacks, who were later to be characterized as the "underclass."[61]

As more and more whites fled to the suburbs and more blacks began turning inward, replacing the Civil Rights Movement's ideology of integration with "black power," "black community control," and general black empowerment, less time and energy were spent worrying about racial integration. As blacks became majorities in major cities of the nation, they began electing black city councillors and black mayors. In 1967, Richard G. Hatcher and Carl B. Stokes, of Gary, Indiana, and Cleveland, Ohio, respectively, became the first elected black mayors of major cities in the United States. But as before in this age of mixed blessings and tragic historical contradictions and gross ironies, this was also the year of the worst urban riot or rebellion in U.S. history, the Detroit riot.[62]

As more black mayors were elected by increasingly black majorities and with the help of some very dedicated whites, suburban whites became increasingly isolated from the black-controlled cities with their rising problems of poverty, crime, and violence. Blacks conversely, began thinking increasingly of suburban whites as the enemy who abandoned the city rather than live under black political power. No love was lost in many cities as these two polarized communities went their separate ways. Detroit is a good example of this racial polarization; as Detroit became blacker and poorer, white suburbanites regularly criticized the city, especially to new white arrivals. As one such "new white arrival," Robert McCabe, president of Detroit Renaissance, explained in 1985, "I'd find people who had their tremendous sense of pride that they haven't been in downtown Detroit in 15 years and don't intend to go."[63] Recognizing this historic pattern of white racism, many black city officials have long since given up on suburban whites as incorrigible racists, and instead have concentrated on building and consolidating black political and economic power in the space that they control. With such conditions prevailing around the country, there seems little hope for bringing blacks and whites together. The tragedy is that both black-majority cities and white-majority suburbs do not and cannot long exist or develop to their fullest potential without regional equity and racial unity.

Contemporary Racial Problems

During the last decade or so, we have faced both new and old racial problems. White resistance to affirmative action has triggered black resentment. Conflicts between blacks and Jews (old and trusted allies during many battles against racism) have caused much bitterness and vitiated the very core of the

---

61. For a working definition of the black underclass, see, Wilson, 6-8.

62. Jaynes and Williams, 69.

63. *Detroit News*, January 8, 1985.

traditional black/white alliance that produced the greatest progress in race relations in twentieth-century American history. Interracial violence in cities like Detroit and New York, between Middle-Eastern merchants and blacks, and Korean merchants and blacks, respectively, complicated the already protracted black/white racial conflicts. Racial conflicts on college campuses reflect the racial tensions in the larger society.[64] Countless people are searching for answers and solutions to America's most persistent social problem. Many have given up hope of ever finding answers or solutions, but there can be no lasting social peace and progress without social justice and racial unity and harmony. Here again, the tragedy is that far too many white- and black-Americans do not realize that there really is no choice: either they learn to live together for the benefit of the *entire* society, or they continue the protracted divisive struggle of racism and racial conflict with inevitably negative results.

---

64. Jonathan Kaufman, *Broken Alliance: The Turbulent Times between Blacks and Jews in America* (New York: New American Library, 1988).

Lowell Cauffiel, "Conflict of Cultures: Blacks and Chaldeans," *The Detroit News*, April 14, 1983, 1a, 11a; Don Terry, "Diplomacy Fails to End Boycott of Korean's Store," *New York Times*, July 16, 1990.

Part III

The Interracial Struggle for Racial Justice, Unity, and Fellowship

CHAPTER 6

THE OTHER TRADITION
IN AMERICAN RACE RELATIONS

I have a dream that one day on the red hills of Georgia, sons of former slaves and sons of former slave-owners will be able to sit down together. . .in Alabama, little black boys and black girls will be able to join hands with little white boys and white girls as sisters and brothers. I have a dream today! . . . With this faith we will be able to transform the jangling discords of our nation into a beautiful symphony of brotherhood.

With this faith we will be able to work together, to pray together, to struggle together, to go to jail together, to stand up for freedom together, knowing that we will be free one day.

Dr. Martin Luther King,Jr.

Understanding the Other Tradition

The long and terrible tradition of racism and racial conflict in the United States has prevented many concerned people from examining the other tradition of American race relations that has embodied the best of American thinking and vision concerning a multiracial society. While far from what we in the 1990s would call "progressive" race relations, this tradition not only challenged the more popular tradition of white racism during each stage of its development but also at the same time held before the eyes of the larger society the vision of a multiracial society based upon racial justice, unity, and cooperation. It did not emerge fully defined, rather it stumbled along, sometimes losing its way, and always struggling to overcome the influences of the stronger tradition of racism; yet, it is this other tradition that has paved the way to a greater vision of a society free of racism and full of human love and fellowship.

This positive tradition started in part with religious communities such as the Quakers in the eighteenth century and can be seen operating today among a wide range of interracial groups and organizations. Many of the contemporary organizations, movements, and religions have infused this tradition with their own individual "spirit" and philosophy, without which infusion this tradition would have long since died out. For example, while the Quakers most certainly ignited and sustained much of this tradition during the early years of slavery, other groups and organizations, such as the early biracial NAACP and Urban League, tapped into the tradition and carried it forward well into the twentieth century. The American Bahá'í community, whose central teachings emphasize racial unity, fellowship, and love, infused a powerful and longlasting spirit into this tradition that is still at work throughout the nation in hundreds of communities. And of course, the Civil Rights Movement and Dr. Martin Luther King Jr.'s philosophy of love and fellowship opened up wider possibilities of multiracial unity and cooperation for a entire generation of blacks and whites.

Notwithstanding the periodic racial conflicts in our cities, on campuses and elsewhere—incidences that receive most if not all of the media coverage, a perhaps understandable tendency given that people often want to hear and see only the worst side of American race relations—this other tradition has never ceased. Badly overshadowed by the louder and more dramatic tradition of racism and racial conflict, this other tradition is slowly making itself felt in many areas of society, in music, art, politics, education, friendship and family networks, and religious communities. It is this tradition that has the power truly to transform our society and to create lasting bonds of genuine love and fellowship among our racially and culturally diverse people.

Turning to this other tradition of race relations should not be seen as denying the still very serious racial problems that face America and the world. Rather, it should be seen as an exploration of those racial experiences in American history that can best teach us how to create racial unity based upon justice, love, and fellowship. We already know a lot about racism and racial conflicts. We know why many whites have traditionally hated and feared nonwhites. We know why, based on the tradition of white racism, many nonwhites dislike and mistrust whites. We also know the tremendous historical and social costs racism and racial conflicts have exacted from the larger society over the centuries. If we know anything about racism and racial conflict, it is this: social progress for the entire society has always been retarded when these two forces have held sway. Racism created the enslavement, segregation, and ghettoization of blacks and the conquest and demoralization of Native peoples; now both groups' present social and economic plight has retarded both their and the larger society's social progress. Where racial justice, love, and fellowship have prevailed, all members of society have progressed. We have only to examine those situations in American history where these positive social factors have prevailed to be convinced. Therefore, we explore and study the other more positive, uplifting tradition of American race relations to understand better what we need to do to create conditions conducive to racial justice, unity, and fellowship. This approach to American race relations has been inspired in part by the late psychologist Abraham Malsow, who transformed the field of psychology by his emphasis on studying "good people" instead of limiting himself to the Freudian model with its emphasis upon studying "sick people."[1]

This other tradition will provide us with a knowledge base for building a "good" multiracial society. It embodies the greatest potential for understanding the historical relationship between racial justice and unity, love, fellowship, and social progress.

---

1. Edward Hoffman, *The Right To Be Human: A Biography of Abraham Maslow* (Los Angeles: Jeremy P. Tarcher, 1988) 151-75, passim.

Seeds of the Tradition: Anti-Slavery Advocates and the Growth and Development of Interracial Cooperation in the Struggle for Racial Justice

No other white religious or secular organization, institution, or group was as committed to ridding itself of slavery as were the early American Quakers. George Fox, the founder of the Society of Friends known as Quakers, very early on wrote to Quaker missionaries in the New World concerning the issue of slavery. In 1657, he warned them about the temptation to enslave blacks and Indians. While he did not attack slavery as such, he made it clear that all people were equal in the sight of God.[2] This would become the first step in a great tradition of American race relations. William Edmundson, an Irish Quaker, became the first Quaker during the American colonial period to attack slavery. Writing to the Friends in 1675 in several slaveholding colonies, Edmundson criticized the ownership of slaves among the Quakers. Before long the Quakers became the leading voice in the attacks on slavery. Their best-known protest against slavery occurred in 1688 in Germantown, known in history as "The Germantown Protest." This statement was drafted by Dutch-speaking Quakers who opposed slavery because of their own persecution in the sixteenth century. This protest did not appear in print until 1844.[3] From the Germantown Protest to the early nineteenth century, the Quakers stood almost alone among American religious groups in circulating published criticisms of slavery.[4]

Colonial Quakers had such strong feelings against African slavery that by 1776 they had "effectively abolished it among themselves."[5] Influenced in large part by John Woolman, who in 1743, "suddenly recognized his aversion to human slavery when he was asked to write a bill of sale for a Negro."[6] These early Quakers became the first among white Americans who refused to compromise their spiritual principles to support and maintain the enslavement of black people. Woolman, however, went further than most Quakers, who as a group were morally far ahead of their white contemporaries. He deeply empathized with the plight of black slaves, an empathy that represented one of the first genuine examples of racial bonding with black humanity, so different from the apologetic racism of people like Thomas Jefferson. Woolman had this to say of black slavery:

Let us calmly consider their Circumstances; and, the better to do it, make their Case ours. Suppose then, that our Ancestors and we had been exposed to constant Servitudes, in the more servile and inferior Employments of

---

2.   Wood, 277.

3.   Wood, 278.

4.   Wood, 278.

5.   Jordan, 114.

6.   Jordan, 114.

Life. . .that while others, in Ease, have plentifully heaped up the Fruit of our Labour, we had receiv'd barely enough to relieve Nature, and being wholly at the Command of others, had generally been treated as a contemptible, ignorant Part of Mankind: Should we, in that Case, be less abject than they are now? [7]

Unlike those in the tradition of American racism, Woolman highlighted the "crushing effects of slavery upon the enslaved."[8] He could have stopped there, with empathy for the slaves, but he was moved to explore how whites first victimized and dehumanized blacks and then held in contempt what they themselves had created. Woolman recognized how slavery produced the white racial attitudes and beliefs.[9]

Anthony Benezet, another Quaker and close friend of Woolman, was "the most prolific of all Quaker antislavery writers."[10] More important, however, Benezet played a major role in expanding the concern for blacks beyond merely seeking justice for slaves to working on their behalf once they were freed. In 1750, Benezet established an evening school for black children in his home and operated the school for twenty years. In June of 1758, he wrote a letter to John Smith criticizing the unfair treatment of the Minisink Indians at the hands of both Quakers and non-Quakers. As historian Forrest G. Wood said of Benezet, "To this Quaker, every human was a child of God. "[11]

Quakers continued to play a key role in the struggle against slavery well into the middle of the nineteenth century. Levin Coffin, a Quaker, became one of the most effective white workers on the Underground Railroad, which depended heavily upon interracial cooperation and trust. Located in southern Indiana, Coffin assisted more than three-thousand slaves to escape to the North.[12]

The Quakers were not perfect by any means. Their founder, George Fox, while cautioning Quakers about the effects of slavery, "accepted Negro slavery as an institution that could be rationalized by the ancient dualisms of body and soul, matter and spirit."[13] But, other Quakers more than made up for the shortcomings of their fellows. Without their contribution, the tradition of interracial cooperation within the anti-slavery movement would have been much less successful.

---

7. Quoted in Jordan, 114.

8. Jordan, 114.

9. Jordan, 115.

10. Wood, 279.

11. Wood, 279-80.

12. Franklin and Mosse, 170; Larry Gara, *The Liberty Line: The Legend of the Underground Railroad* (Lexington: University of Kentucky Press, 1967) 94-95.

13. Wood, 77.

Between the 1830s and the start of the Civil War, the anti-slavery movement provided the major impetus for interracial cooperation. Notwithstanding the ideological conflicts that sometimes emerged between white abolitionists and black abolitionists, the movement itself constituted the most advanced form of interracial cooperation up to that time in American history. Whites and blacks risked their lives assisting slaves to freedom. Whites who worked on the Underground Railroad had very little to gain, and their lives and property to lose. Blacks expanded whites' vision of what America could become when free of slavery and racism and infused with interracial vigor. Whites and blacks, men and women forged a new interracial identity as they worked together and independently to end slavery. Whatever the shortcomings in their relationships at that stage of interracial cooperation, it was a small price to pay for the contribution of their joint efforts to move America a little closer to a multiracial society based on justice, love, and fellowship.[14]

During the Civil War black soldiers and white officers in the Union Army found themselves involved in an interracial alliance that had the potential both to strengthen or weaken the tradition of interracial cooperation for racial justice. Many white union officers held the same racist views of blacks as the white southerners they were fighting, and their views of the purpose of the war were quite different from those of the black men under their command: whites were fighting to reunite the country, while blacks were fighting to end the enslavement of their people. While not always mutually exclusive, these two racial visions posed difficult problems for interracial cooperation. Yet, in the long run, due to shared dangers and daily interaction and genuine mutual concerns, a significant degree of racial bonding occurred among the men. This bonding sensitized many white union officers to the humanity of black people and provided blacks, many of whom had been slaves, with an opportunity to interact with some white officers who genuinely believed in racial justice and equality. This interracial cooperation (unfortunately forged on some of the bloodiest battlefields of the war) revealed both to the men and to the larger society an example of interracial cooperation unprecedented in American history.[15]

The Tradition and New Challenge during the Post-Slavery Period

The emancipation of southern black slaves in January of 1863 represented the finest fruit of the long tradition of struggle for racial justice. Not even the facts that the Emancipation Proclamation was in large part a war measure, was

---

14.   Vincent Harding, *There is a River: The Black Struggle for Freedom in America* (New York: Harcourt Brace Jovanovich, 1981) 124-29;   Benjamin Quarles, *Black Abolitionists* (New York: Oxford University Press, 1969) 49-50, 56, 235;   Robert L. Allen, *Reluctant Reformers: Racism and Social Reform Movements in the United States* (Garden City, New York: Doubleday and Co., Anchor Edition, 1975) 31-49.

15.   Joseph T. Glatthaar, *Forged in Battle: The Civil War Alliance of Black Soldiers and White Officers* (New York: The Free Press, 1990) 99-169.

opposed in some powerful and influential circles both in the United States and abroad, and was originally connected with serious thoughts of the colonization of emancipated slaves beyond the limits of the U.S. could taint its historic meaning for those who had struggled for so long to end the enslavement of black people.[16] To many white abolitionists the end of slavery meant the end of the struggle for racial justice. Others, however, realizing that freeing slaves was only a step in the still long journey towards racial justice and unity, continued to expand the agenda of the racial justice tradition. They realized the Emancipation Proclamation did not grant blacks the rights and protections of citizens. Therefore, they began struggling for the passage of the Thirteenth Amendment, which outlawed slavery, and the Fourteenth and Fifteenth Amendments, which made blacks citizens and gave black males the right to vote. Not all white abolitionists agreed with this expanded agenda because it forced the question of the extent to which abolitionism advocated and supported full racial equality for the emancipated blacks. Those white abolitionists who had the larger vision and the longer view on the tradition of racial justice would not even stop with the passage of the three Amendments. They were among those hundreds of whites and blacks who went to the South to teach and provide economic assistance to the former slaves.[17]

By 1870 this tradition of struggle for racial justice and the fostering of interracial cooperation was beginning to wane among even its most ardent supporters. The Radical Republicans and former abolitionists felt they had done all they could for the cause by attaining the passage of the Fourteenth and Fifteenth Amendments. As far as they were concerned, they had paid their dues. The anti-slavery societies closed down and advised their members to continue the tradition of struggling for racial justice by working either as individuals or with new organizations to eliminate racism in both the South and the North. Some began working on integrating schools, a struggle that would last almost a century in many areas of the country.[18] Less than a decade later, the country was back to business as usual, and the tradition of racial justice, unity, and cooperation was under siege. Various forms of interracial cooperation emerged between the end of Reconstruction and the first decade of the twentieth century. However, most of them tended either to have short lifespans or to use interracial cooperation as a means to maintain new forms of white racial dominance. For example, the southern Populist movement succeeded for a while in creating interracial unity and cooperation between black farmers and white farmers. Georgia Populist leader Tom Watson recognized how racism kept the black and the white farmers fighting each other while the ruling elites exploited them both. Writing in 1892, Watson explained the basis of this mutual oppression:

---

16.   John Hope Franklin, *The Emancipation Proclamation* (Garden City, New York: Doubleday & Company, Anchor Books, 1965) 68-69, 81, 129-30.

17.   Allen, 46.

18.   Allen, 47.

You are kept apart that you may be separately fleeced of your earnings. You are made to hate each other because upon that hatred is rested the keystone of the arch of financial despotism which enslaves you both. You are deceived and blinded that you may not see how this race antagonism perpetuates a monetary system which beggars both. [19]

Watson was one of the first white leaders in the South to attempt to articulate a social philosophy of interracial cooperation and unity, but he based it on the most tenuous of bonds: self-interest. "Gratitude may fail: so may sympathy and friendship and generosity and patriotism; but in the long run, self-interest always controls."[20] Mutual racial self-interest, Watson believed, was the rock upon which interracial cooperation and unity could best be built and sustained:

Let it once appear plainly that it is to the interests of a colored man to vote with the white man, and he will do it. Let it plainly appear that it is to the interest of the white man that the vote of the Negro should supplement his own, and the question of having that ballot freely cast and fairly counted becomes vital to the white man.[21]

According to Watson, the People's Party (Populism's political arm) constituted the best instrument through which this interracial self-interest could express itself. But Watson, as Allen has pointed out so well, was only interested in interracial cooperation and unity as a means of "paternalistic pragmatism." Since blacks were a significant portion of the southern population and could not be ignored, they had to be accommodated. White racial self-interest in such circumstances, therefore, dictated that blacks be included in the movement. While "white southern Populists attacked certain racist practices detrimental to the growth of the political power, they did not challenge the underlying ideology of white supremacy—and in the long run this was to prove their undoing."[22]

The southern Populist form of interracial cooperation and unity represented one of the weakest of all historical forms of interracial unity and cooperation. Had white Populists and black Populists been able to develop a deeper, stronger bond based on genuine concern for each other's common humanity, they might have sustained their unity. But partisan power politics determined the nature of interracial cooperation and unity during much of this period. By 1896 Populism had passed from the scene, and when Tom Watson reemerged in 1904, he was advocating the disenfranchisement of southern blacks.[23]

---

19. Norman Pollack, ed., *The Populist Mind* (Indianapolis and New York: Bobbs-Merrill Company, 1967) 371-72.

20. Pollack, 369-70.

21. Pollack, 369-70.

22. Allen, 53.

23. Allen, 79.

For a while Tom Watson had tapped into the positive tradition of American race relations, that of interracial struggle for racial justice, even if wrapped in racial political expediency. Was not the Emancipation Proclamation such a racial political expediency as well, one that fortunately turned out well in the end? What is important is that at this stage of American race relations, after centuries of black slavery when many white Americans still found it difficult to conceive of a multiracial democracy or of sharing political power with ex-slaves or blacks who had never been slaves for that matter, any formula of inter-racial cooperation and unity would do. Watson and the southern Populists tried to build a political movement upon a form of racial mutual self-interest. This effort failed because the tradition of white supremacy proved much stronger than the watered-down tradition of racial political expediency that Watson and the southern Populists attempted to substitute for the more spiritually powerful tradition of the interracial struggle for racial justice, unity, and fellowship.

Other white social movements also failed to develop genuine interracial cooperation and unity because of this tendency to compromise spiritual princi-ples for short-term political, economic, and social gains for whites only. Two other examples from the nineteenth century should suffice to make this point. In the mid-1880s, from among the largest post-Civil War labor organizations, only the Knights of Labor showed genuine willingness to include black workers in their union. Black workers flocked to the Knights. In the South, there were both integrated and segregated Locals. During this period close to sixty-thousand blacks became members of the Knights. The Knights of Labor's motto, "An injury to one is a concern to all," seemed for a short while to be the answer to both class and race oppression. Labor historian Philip S. Foner, com-menting on Knights of Labor's commitment to racial justice and unity, said:

> At its height and at its best, the Knights of Labor had acted upon the words of Frederick Douglass in 1833: "The labor unions of the country should not throw away this colored element of strength. . . .It is a great mistake for any class of laborers to isolate itself and thus weaken the bond of brotherhood between those on whom the burden and hardships of labor falls."[24]

In 1886, a white member of the Knights of Labor wrote in his book entitled *The Great Labor Question, or The Noble Mission of the Knights of Labor*: "Perhaps one of the noblest acts of the Knights of Labor, is that of rising above the prejudices of thousands and millions of people that were engendered against the negro race when they were in bondage."[25] "At its best" the Knights stood squarely in the heart of the best and highest tradition of American race relations and its "noblest act" of "rising above the prejudices" of millions of whites reflected the best of that great tradition. But like the Populists the Knights did not sufficiently inoculate themselves against the virus of racism. ". . .[T]he

---

24. Foner, 63.

25. Quoted in Foner, 63.

Knights contributed immensely toward a brief era of good feelings between black and white workingmen, even in the South." However, Foner continues, "From these heights the Knights of Labor steadily declined, year after year weakening the fraternal bonds it had built, until at the end it became an apologist for white supremacy."[26]

The tradition was powerful when grounded in the principles of true racial unity. However, racial compromise and expediency, elements of the tradition of racism, eroded these principles and in the long run retarded both the growth and development of racial justice, cooperation, unity, and fellowship as well as social progress for society at large. By compromising the full expression of the best tradition of American race relations, these organizations prevented the full flowering of human potential latent in the multiracial composition of American society.

The first decade of the twentieth century witnessed what one historian of the NAACP has called the "Reincarnation of the Abolitionists."[27] Called into action by the increasingly racist social and political climate, the NAACP formed in 1909 from the merger of two major groups: the all-black Niagara Movement led by W.E.B. DuBois, and a group of concerned whites led by a young white social worker Mary White Ovington. In 1909 both groups met in New York in a National Negro Conference. Within a year, they formed the NAACP, which was destined to become the oldest civil rights movement in the United States. A year later, another biracial organization, the National League on Urban Conditions among Negroes (Urban League) emerged, as part of the tradition of racial justice, cooperation, and unity. While the NAACP's role was limited to the struggle to secure civil and political rights for blacks, the Urban League's role was to focus on the economic uplifting of black workers in urban areas. In 1911, they arrived at a tacit agreement that each would work in its own area of concern.[28]

Against the backdrop of racism, the NAACP and Urban League represented two of the best models of the tradition of racial justice, cooperation, unity, and fellowship. Free of the racial compromise and expediency of the Populists and Knights of Labor, the NAACP's and Urban League's major goals centered around the political, social, and economic advancement of black people. The goals and objectives of both organizations stimulated formal and informal interaction between blacks and whites. This contributed to building trust, fellowship, and lasting friendships among members. This is not to say that conflicts related to race, ideology, and tactics did not occur within these two pioneer biracial organizations. For example, the resignation of W.E.B. DuBois in 1934 and the subsequent conflicts between young black radicals and older white liberals over

---

26. Foner, 63.

27. Barbara Joyce Ross, *J.E.Spingarn and the Rise of the NAACP, 1911-1939* (New York: Atheneum, 1972) 17-19.

28. Langston Hughes, *Fight for Freedom: The Story of the NAACP* (New York: W.W. Norton & Company, 1963) 17-21, 31, 186-87.

tactics caused much concern but did not destroy future interracial cooperation within the organization. During the Civil Rights Era, NAACP units "formed interracial picket lines of both old and young," both black- and white-NAACP lawyers worked together to secure racial justice. Out of this devotion to racial justice emerged genuine bonds of friendship and love that demonstrated to a sceptical world the power of a tradition devoted to racial justice, unity, coopera-tion, and fellowship. However, the bonds were constantly being tested by both internal and external social forces. In the summer of 1964 long-time NAACP lawyer, Jack Greenberg and some blacks in Mississippi clashed over his role as a white in the Civil Rights Movement. According to Kaufman, during the 1970s, some black lawyers resented Greenberg's role as head of the NAACP Legal Defense Fund.[29]

While the NAACP presented a model of interracial cooperation and unity in the struggle for racial justice for blacks, their work was complemented by the National Urban League, which represented a model of interracial cooperation for the economic uplifting of blacks in urban communities. Inspired by the spirit of the progressive movement, black and white social reformers struggled separately and jointly to help southern black migrants survive in the industrial North. But not until the founding of the National Urban League (NUL) in New York in 1911, through the merger of three other related organizations—the Committee on Urban Conditions among Negroes in New York, the National League for the Protection of Colored Women, and the Committee for Improving Industrial Conditions among Negroes—did a really effective national program dedicated to black urban survival emerge.[30] While the NUL failed to solve many of the major problems plaguing black urban America, it did provide a safety net without which many black workers and their families would not have survived. Much like the NAACP, it brought together dedicated social reformers and professionals to address the problems of urban blacks. The NUL embodied many of the tradition's best aspects of interracial cooperation as it gradually developed a nationwide network of blacks and whites from which it could tap resources to solve black urban problems. This network included capitalist-philanthropists such as Julius Rosenwald, Jr.; John D. Rockefeller, Jr.; Ruth Standish Baldwin; Alfred White; and a generation of very bright and profes-sionally trained black social workers.[31] As in most other evolving biracial organizations during this period, interracial cooperation and unity often became tied to larger social and economic agendas of the more powerful white players. Two scholars writing in the 1930s understood this relationship when they wrote: "Many of the largest industrial concerns came to regard the local league as a useful agency for procuring labor and as a conservative stabilizing force in

---

29. Hughes, 122-23; Ross, 186-245; Kaufman, 109.

30. Nancy J. Weiss, *The National Urban League:1910-1940* (New York: Oxford University Press, 1974) 41-46.

31. Weiss, 41-46; Hollingsworth Wood, "The Urban League Movement," *The Journal of Negro History* 9 (April, 1924): 119-20.

the colored community, and contributed substantially to its support."[32] However often these kinds of obviously exploitative elements might have crept into the work of the NUL with powerful economic forces, they did not alter the essential purpose and objectives of generations of black and white social workers who carried on the tradition of interracial cooperation and unity in their work.[33]

Throughout the 1930s, several reform and labor movements preached interracial solidarity. Socialists, Communists, and the Congress of Industrial Organizations (CIO) began working in various ways and (for as many reasons and motives) for interracial unity. The labor movement, of which the CIO was the most progressive on racial issues, had come to realize the power of racial cooperation and unity. Unfortunately, they had not learned very much since the days of the Knights of Labor: their interest in unity between blacks and whites was largely limited to class issues. Blacks were seen as essential to the unionization of the mass production industrial plants. But the vast majority of white workers were not interested in racial unity beyond the shop floor. However, in all fairness to the CIO, many of its international unions, such as the United Auto Workers, made major contributions to the long struggle for racial justice, cooperation, and unity. Not unlike other biracial organizations of the twentieth century, they built long-term bonds and alliances that greatly expanded and strengthened the tradition of racial unity and cooperation.[34]

During the next several decades, the tradition of racial justice, cooperation, unity, and fellowship clashed on many fronts with the tradition of racial hatred, conflict, and polarization. From the 1940s to the late 1960s, the latter tradition fought the former tradition in every area of social, political, and economic life. It was a war for the heart and soul of America. At the height of the Civil Rights Movement, blacks and whites reached one of the highest stages of interracial cooperation, unity, and spiritual fellowship ever achieved in the history of American race relations. But under the stress, conflicts, and confusion of the time, it all came apart, evaporated in pain and anguish and distrust. What was once called the "beloved community" faded away as many blacks and whites went their separate ways, concerned only with their separate agendas. Once again, something quite basic was missing: a spiritual force strong enough to sustain the long and difficult growth of building genuine interracial fellowship. At the present time, there are still organizations and groups working for racial justice, cooperation, unity, and fellowship, but there are few interracial communities that have been established for the sole purpose of the unification of the human race and that see racial justice, cooperation, unity, and fellowship as essential elements of this process.

---

32.   Sterling D. Spero and Abram L. Harris, *The Black Worker* (New York: Columbia University Press, 1931) 141.

33.   Several good local examples of this long tradition of interracial cooperation can still be seen in such local Urban League branches as Lansing and Detroit in Michigan.

34.   Sumner M. Rosen, "The CIO Era, 1935-55," in Jacobson, 188-208.

CHAPTER 7

TOWARDS A MODEL OF RACIAL
UNITY: BAHÁ'Í TEACHINGS
AND COMMUNITY PRACTICES

My hope is that the white and the black will be united in perfect love and fellowship, with complete unity and brotherhood. Associate with each other, think of each other, and be like a rose garden. Anyone who goes into a rose garden will see various roses, white, pink, yellow, red, all growing together and replete with adornment. Each one accentuates the beauty of the other. . . .I hope you will continue in unity and fellowship. How beautiful to see blacks and whites together! I hope, God willing, the day may come when I shall see the red men, the Indians, with you, Japanese and others. Then there will be white roses, yellow roses, red roses, and a very wonderful rose garden will appear in the world.

'Abdu'l-Bahá, *Promulgation of Universal Peace*

One other pattern deserves mention. Though the process of achieving racial harmony involves all the races in the human family, it is the unity of black and white that American Bahá'ís are asked to give special attention. The legacy of distrust between these two races casts a shadow that only the light of unity can dispel. Consequently, the power of unity between black and white serves to draw all the other racial and cultural minorities into its embrace. We cannot afford to ignore the special blessings that come from fostering the unity of black and white.

National Race Unity Committee
Bahá'ís of the United States, *The Power of Unity*

The Bahá'í Teachings on Racial Unity: A New Approach to American Race Relations History

As we have seen, the history of the interracial struggle for racial justice, unity, and cooperation in the United States has experienced both great advances and equally great setbacks. Somehow even the most ardent and ambitious movements for racial justice have tended to burn out, to regress into racism and compromise, or to abandon outright the vision of a just, loving multiracial society, and turned inward to concentrate on more "practical" social programs. Not even veteran civil-rights organizations such as the NAACP and CORE have been spared the grinding and demoralizing effects of the protracted interracial struggle to achieve a multiracial society based upon justice, love, trust, and cooperation. Given the long and noble tradition of the interracial struggle to achieve a just and loving society, what went wrong? Has racism been so virulent that it has poisoned the entire body-politic and spiritual core of present-day American society? Is it possible that racism and racial conflicts are social maladies we will just have to learn to live with, or just "manage"?

There are some very basic historical reasons why the various movements, organizations, and individuals that have contributed so much to the tradition of racial justice, unity, and cooperation have not been able to effect a longer-lasting positive transformation of American race relations. One reason is the historically persistent and adaptive nature of racism among many white Americans and their inability or unwillingness to see such racism as a chronic social, psychological, and spiritual illness that retards their own healthy growth and development as well as that of racial minorities and the larger society. In addition, the deep-seated mistrust, suspicion, and bitterness among black Americans that flow from the history of white racism will have to be eliminated. Another reason is the repeated failure and unwillingness of many well-meaning individuals, organizations, and movements within the noble tradition of the interracial struggle for racial justice, unity, cooperation, and fellowship, to explore the vast potential of spiritual approaches to the problem. As a result, those persons, groups, and organizations that have contributed so much to the tradition have been unable to infuse in the tradition the necessary spirit and vision to effect a lasting transformation in racial attitudes and behavior. The erratic advances and reverses in the history of American race relations are due in large part to this lack of a unifying spirit and vision of racial love and fellowship that can bond people and set their hearts and souls on fire to create a truly harmonious multiracial community.

Long-term racial transformation can only occur within a community dedicated to interracial love, fellowship, and unity. Nothing less will suffice. A community of loving, caring, nurturing human beings will not only be able to address the issue of racial justice but will also move far beyond that stage to more transcendent stages of interracial love, unity, and fellowship. Such an interracial community would create a synergistic interracial force that would in turn not only transform race relations but also transform countless other social relationships in the United States. The entire social and economic order of the United States would be transformed if blacks and whites became spiritually unified. In addition, this spiritual unity would contribute to the spiritual unification of the entire planet. As 'Abdu'l-Bahá (1844-1921), the son of the founder of the Bahá'í Faith and its head from 1892-1921, explained during his visit to the United States in 1912, "When the racial elements of the American nation unite in actual fellowship and accord, the lights of the oneness of humanity will shine, the day of eternal glory and bliss will dawn, the spirit of God encompass, and the divine favors descend."[1]

---

1. 'Abdu'l-Bahá, *Promulgation of Universal Peace*, 2d ed., comp. Howard MacNutt (Wilmette: Bahá'í Publishing Trust, 1982) 57.

The Bahá'í teachings on racial unity emanate from a larger wealth of teachings by Bahá'u'lláh (1817-92), the Prophet-Founder of the Faith, on the unity of the human race. The principle of unity stands at the very heart of Bahá'u'lláh's revelation and the Bahá'í community life:

Ye are all the leaves of one tree and the drops of one ocean.[2]

O CHILDREN OF MEN! Know ye not why We created you all from the same dust? That no one should exalt himself over the other. Ponder at all times in your hearts how ye were created. Since We have created you all from one same substance it is incumbent on you to be even as one soul, to walk with the same feet, eat with the same mouth and dwell in the same land, that from your inmost being, by your deeds and actions, the signs of oneness and the essence of detachment may be made manifest. Such is My counsel to you, O concourse of light! Heed ye this counsel that ye may obtain the fruit of holiness from the tree of wondrous glory.[3]

He Who is your Lord, the All-Merciful, cherisheth in His heart the desire of beholding the entire human race as one soul and one body.[4]

'Abdu'l-Bahá explained the meaning of unity in these words:

What is real unity? When we observe the human world, we find various collective expressions of unity therein. For instance, man is distinguished from the animal by his degree, or kingdom. This comprehensive distinction includes all the posterity of Adam and constitutes one great household or human family, which may be considered the fundamental or physical unity of mankind. Furthermore, a distinction exists between various groups of humankind according to lineage, each group forming a racial unity separate from the others. There is also the unity of tongue among those who use the same language as a means of communication; national unity where various people live under one form of government such as French, German, British, etc.; and political unity, which conserves the civil rights of parties or factions of the same government. All these unities are imaginary and without real foundation, for no real result proceeds from them. The purpose of true unity is real and divine outcomes. From these limited unities mentioned only limited outcomes proceed, whereas unlimited unity produces unlimited result. For instance, from the limited unity of race or nationality the results at most are limited. It is like a family living alone and solitary; there are no unlimited or universal outcomes from it.

The unity which is productive of unlimited results is first a unity of mankind which recognizes that all are sheltered beneath the overshadowing

---

2. Bahá'u'lláh, *Tablets of Bahá'u'lláh Revealed after Kitáb-i-Aqdas*, comp. Research Department, trans. H. Taherzadeh (Haifa: Bahá'í World Centre, 1978) 129.

3. Bahá'u'lláh, *The Hidden Words of Bahá'u'lláh*, trans. Shoghi Effendi (Wilmette: Bahá'í Publishing Trust, 1975) 20.

4. Bahá'u'lláh, *Gleanings from the Writings of Bahá'u'lláh* trans. Shoghi Effendi (Wilmette: Bahá'í Publishing Trust, 1952) 214.

glory of the All-Glorious, that all are servants of one God; for all breathe the same atmosphere, live upon the same earth, move beneath the same heavens, receive effulgence from the same sun and are under the protection of one God. This is the most great unity, and its results are lasting if humanity adheres to it; but mankind has hitherto violated it, adhering to sectarian or other limited unities such as racial, patriotic or unity of self-interests; therefore, no great results have been forthcoming. Nevertheless, it is certain that the radiance and favors of God are encompassing, minds have developed, perceptions have become acute, sciences and arts are widespread, and capacity exists for the proclamation and promulgation of the real and ultimate unity of mankind, which will bring forth marvelous results. It will reconcile all religions, make warring nations loving, cause hostile kings to become friendly and bring peace and happiness to the human world. It will cement together the Orient and Occident, remove forever the foundations of war and upraise the ensign of the Most Great Peace.[5]

The lack of this "most great unity" has prevented the world from solving many of its most intractable problems. Along with the need for unity among all the peoples of the world is the need for true love among human beings. "The disease which afflicts the body politic is lack of love and absence of altruism," 'Abdu'l-Bahá explained. "In the hearts of men no real love is found, and the condition is such that, unless their susceptibilities are quickened by some power so that unity, love and accord may develop within them, there can be no healing, no agreement among mankind." It is clear, then, according to 'Abdu'l-Bahá, that "love and unity are the needs of the body politic today. Without these there can be no progress or prosperity attained. Therefore, the friends of God must adhere to the power which will create this love and unity in the hearts of the sons of men."[6]

It is difficult for even the most secure and well-meaning social reformers and the average concerned citizen to grasp this simple truth: love, fellowship, and unity are inseparable from the social advancement of the entire human race. "It is certain that the greatest of instrumentalities for achieving the advancement and the glory of man, the supreme agency for the enlightenment and the redemption of the world," 'Abdu'l-Bahá counselled, "is love and fellowship and unity among all the members of the human race. Nothing can be effected in the world, not even conceivably, without unity and agreement, and the perfect means for engendering fellowship and union is true religion."[7]

In this very secular world with its overreliance on science, politics, war, and revolution as key instrumentalities of social change, this emphasis upon "true religion" as "the perfect means for engendering fellowship and union" is often

---

5. *Promulgation* 190-91.

6. *Promulgation* 171.

7. 'Abdu'l-Bahá, *Secrets of Divine Civilization,* 3d ed., trans. Marzieh Gail (Wilmette: Bahá'í Publishing Trust, 1975) 73.

summarily dismissed as too simpleminded and naive. But few can deny at this stage of human history that the world is undergoing a process of fragmentation on every level of social, political, and economic life. And that even the present hopeful signs of world unification cannot be sustained without some unifying force capable of not only overcoming the countless divisions among humankind but also elevating it to higher levels of unity and cooperation. "Naught but the celestial potency of the Word of God, which ruleth and transcendeth the realities of all things, is capable of harmonizing the divergent thoughts, sentiments, ideas, and convictions of the children of men." 'Abdu'l Bahá again explained. "Verily, it is the penetrating power in all things, the mover of souls and the binder and regulator in the world of humanity."[8]

This spiritual power spoken of in the Bahá'í writings is none other than that "force" or spiritual power spoken of in all the great spiritual traditions of the world. We have seen it operating throughout the history of humankind, called different names by different religions. The world has seen and felt the influence of this "penetrating power" that has moved souls and bonded divergent peoples and nations. However much some arrogant secular minds might want to deny it, this powerful spiritual force has influenced the history of humankind in ways that we have only just begun to understand. All the great Prophets spoke of this force, and all the great spiritual movements testified to the elevating power of this penetrating force. As in other religious traditions, the Bahá'í Faith describes this spiritual force as the "Holy Spirit" and Bahá'ís believe that this is "the penetrating power which is capable of creating love and fellowship" among all the members of the human race. 'Abdu'l-Bahá has said:

> Bahá'u'lláh teaches that the world of humanity is in need of the breath of the Holy Spirit, for in spiritual quickening and enlightenment true oneness is attained with God and man. The Most Great Peace cannot be assured through racial force and effort; it cannot be established by patriotic devotion and sacrifice; for nations differ widely and local patriotism has limitations. Furthermore, it is evident that political power and diplomatic ability are not conducive to universal agreement, for the interests of governments are varied and selfish; nor will international harmony and reconciliation be an outcome of human opinions concentrated upon it, for opinions are faulty and intrinsically diverse. Universal peace is an impossibility through human and material agencies; it must be through spiritual power. There is need of a universal impelling force which will establish the oneness of humanity and destroy the foundations of war and strife. None other than the divine power can do this; therefore, it will be accomplished through the breath of the Holy Spirit.[9]

According to the Bahá'í writings, "The Holy Spirit is like unto the life in the human body, which blends all differences of all parts and members in unity and

---

8. 'Abdu'l-Bahá, *Selections from the Writings of 'Abdu'l-Bahá* (Haifa, Bahá'í World Centre, 1978) 292.

9. *Promulgation* 108-9.

agreement" and "establishes such a unity in the bodily organism that if any part is subjected to injury or becomes diseased, all the other parts and functions sympathetically respond and suffer, owing to the perfect oneness existing."[10]

One can hardly imagine the power of such a degree of sympathy among all the members of the human race to contribute to the social and economic well-being of the human family. Such a power would be capable of releasing vast stores of creative energy into every area of human life, healing and elevating the entire human race. It could do all this simply by the process of spiritual unity. "Just as the human spirit of life is the cause of coordination among the various parts of the human organism, the Holy Spirit is the controlling cause of the unity and coordination of mankind." Elaborating further, 'Abdu'l-Bahá comments, "That is to say, the bond or oneness of humanity cannot be effectively established save through the power of the Holy Spirit, for the world of humanity is a composite body, and the Holy Spirit is the animating principle of its life."[11]

Bahá'ís firmly believe in the spiritual power of the Holy Spirit to unite all people in love and fellowship. According to their Writings, ". . .the foundation of real brotherhood. . .the cause of real kindness and unselfish devotion is none other than the breaths of the Holy Spirit." No other influences, according to the Bahá'í writings, are capable of such a difficult task. "Without this influence and animus it is impossible. We may be able to realize some degrees of fraternity through other motives," 'Abdu'l-Bahá stated, "but these are limited associations and subject to change. When human brotherhood is founded upon the Holy Spirit, it is eternal, changeless, unlimited."[12]

In 1936, almost a hundred years after the founding of the worldwide Bahá'í Faith, Shoghi Effendi (1897-1957), the appointed Guardian of the Faith from 1921-1957, described how a "universal" and "transcending love" among Bahá'ís of diverse backgrounds had "burned away their prejudices" and "made them lovers of mankind." Clearly the Bahá'í belief in the transforming power of the Holy Spirit was at work within their community:

> The Faith of Bahá'u'lláh has assimilated, by virtue of its creative, its regulative and ennobling energies, the varied races, nationalities, creeds and classes that have sought its shadow, and have pledged unswerving fealty to its cause. It has changed the hearts of its adherents, burned away their prejudices, stilled their passions, exalted their conceptions, ennobled their motives, coördinated their efforts, and transformed their outlook. While preserving their patriotism and safeguarding their lesser loyalties, it has made them lovers of mankind, and the determined upholders of its best and truest interests. . . .This universal, this transcending love which the followers of the Bahá'í Faith feel for their fellow-men, of whatever race, creed, class or

---

10. *Promulgation* 321.

11. *Promulgation* 321.

12. *Promulgation* 392.

nation, is neither mysterious nor can it be said to have been artificially stimulated. It is both spontaneous and genuine. They whose hearts are warmed by the energizing influence of God's creative love cherish His creatures for His sake, and recognize in every human face a sign of His reflected glory.[13]

Bahá'ís throughout the world are involved in building an international community of diverse peoples, many from previously mutually antagonistic backgrounds. Once these people became Bahá'ís, they were encouraged to accept all peoples regardless of race, class, or religious differences. So unlike the traditional religious and secular organizations, the Bahá'í teachings did not compromise on the principle of love, unity, and fellowship among its diverse members. At a time when most of the world frowned upon marriage across racial, religious, and cultural boundaries, the Bahá'í teachings encouraged it as one of the highest expressions of unity and love among diverse peoples. 'Abdu'l-Bahá warmly encouraged interracial marriage: "In marriage the more distant the blood-relationship the better, for such distance in family ties between husband and wife provides the basis for the well-being of humanity and is conducive to fellowship among mankind."[14]

In a world faith as diverse as the Bahá'í Faith, Bahá'ís from diverse cultural, religious, and racial backgrounds needed constant encouragement to understand and appreciate the social ramifications of the spiritual teachings of their Faith. Since the Bahá'í teachings embraced intermarriage, rejected by some traditional religions of which they had once been members, many Bahá'ís needed guidance and encouragement on how best to apply the Bahá'í teachings on unity to the traditional problems of intermarriage. Addressing the problem of intermarriage between Zoroastrian and Hindu Bahá'ís, Shoghi Effendi gave this advice:

> With regard to the problem of intermarriage between the Zoroastrian and Hindu Bahá'ís, this is a highly delicate and vital question, as important as the problem of the black and white in America. The friends should all realize that racial considerations do not, in the light of the Bahá'í Teachings, constitute any hindrance to any kind of intercourse between the believers. The Hindu and Zoroastrian Bahá'ís should forget their former and traditional prejudices whether religious, racial or social, and commune together on a common basis of equality, love and devotion to the Cause. While the goal is quite clear yet, wisdom and caution are needed in order to carry this ideal into full practice.[15]

13. Shoghi Effendi, *The World Order of Bahá'u'lláh*, 2d ed. (Wilmette: Bahá'í Publishing Trust, 1974) 197-98.

14. 'Abdu'l-Bahá in Bonnie Taylor, ed., *The Power of Unity: Beyond Prejudice and Racism* (Wilmette: Bahá'í Publishing Trust, 1986) 55.

15. Letter from Shoghi Effendi to individual believer, *Dawn of a New Civilization: Messages to India 1923-1957* (New Delhi, India: Bahá'í Publishing Trust, 1970) 198..

'Abdu'l-Bahá had already demonstrated the Bahá'í teachings reflecting this "ideal" when in 1912 he united a black man and a white woman in marriage and praised their union as a means for promoting "love and affection between the black and white."

> O ye two who have believed in Him!...I pray God that ye may at all times be in the utmost love and harmony, and be a cause for the spirituality of the human world. This union will unquestionably promote love and affection between the black and the white, and will affect and encourage others. These two races will unite and merge together, and there will appear and take root a new generation sound in health and beauteous in countenance.[16]

In a letter written on his behalf in 1957 to the American Bahá'í Inter-racial Teaching Committee, Shoghi Effendi, who was appointed by 'Abdu'l-Bahá to be the Guardian of the Bahá'í Faith (1921-57), told them that "The Bahá'ís should welcome the [N]egroes to their homes, make every effort to teach them, associate with them, even marry them if they want to." He then reminded them of 'Abdu'l-Bahá's encouragement of interracial marriage. "We must remember that 'Abdu'l-Bahá Himself united in Bahá'í marriage a colored and a white believer. He could not do more."[17]

The Bahá'í teachings on racial justice, unity, fellowship, and love have provided the American Bahá'í community with priceless encouragement and guidance throughout its history. No other religious community in American history can lay claim to such a rich tradition of explicit teachings on how to create and maintain a multiracial fellowship. At a time when most Christian denominations were either silent or apologetic about their segregationist practices—practices that still prevail today among the vast majority of American Christians—the American Bahá'í community was being encouraged and guided by the Bahá'í teachings on racial unity. Without such explicit and emphatic guidance on racial unity provided by the central figures of the Bahá'í Faith and later by the appointed Guardian and still later by the world governing body of the Bahá'í Faith, the Universal House of Justice, the American Bahá'í community would have gone the way of the American churches, which compromised on racial justice, fellowship, and unity, to the point where they have currently become the tragic example of one of the most racially segregated institutions in present-day America. Specific Bahá'í teachings and instructions on racial issues saved the American Bahá'í community from the historic fate of the American Christian community.

We have already discussed the Bahá'í teachings on the unity of the human race, the core belief of the Bahá'í Faith and noted how Bahá'ís believe that such unity can only come about through the instrumentality of some spiritual force,

---

16.   'Abdu'l-Bahá in Taylor, *Power of Unity* .

17.   Gayle Morrison, *To Move the World: Louis G. Gregory and the Advancement of Racial Unity in America* (Wilmette: Bahá'í Publishing Trust, 1982) 294.

such as "the Holy Spirit." Furthermore, we have seen how such a belief in the organic unity of the human race accepts and encourages intermarriage among all peoples. Yet, such beliefs have not proceeded without challenges and resistance within the Bahá'í community, particularly within the American Bahá'í community during its long struggle to overcome the influence of racism and racial conflicts among its members. This resistance was overcome due to the clear and emphatic teachings and guidance on race relations provided by the Bahá'í writings.

The most important among the Bahá'í teachings on race have dealt with black/white relations in America. "Intense is the hatred, in America, between black and white, but my hope is that the power of the Kingdom will bind these two in friendship, and serve them as a healing balm." 'Abdu'l-Bahá said, "Let them look not upon a man's color but upon his heart. If the heart be filled with light, that man is nigh unto the threshold of His Lord; but if not, that man is careless of His Lord, be he white or be he black."[18]

Many people of both races simply did not believe that blacks and whites could ever become united. But American Bahá'ís were expected to trust in the power of the Holy Spirit. "To bring the white and the black together is considered impossible and unfeasible, but the breaths of the Holy Spirit will bring about this union." Bahá'ís were expected to trust in this spiritual force working through the Holy Spirit to create harmony between black and white. ". . .[t]he enmity and hatred which exists between the white and the black races is very dangerous and there is no doubt that it will end in bloodshed unless the influence of the Word of God, the breaths of the Holy Spirit and the teachings of Bahá'u'lláh are diffused amongst them and harmony is established between the two races." According to 'Abdu'l-Bahá, "They must destroy the foundation of enmity and rancor and lay the basis of love and affinity. The power of the Teachings of Bahá'u'lláh will remove this danger from America."[19]

Modeling the Bahá'í Teachings on Racial Unity, Love, and Fellowship: 'Abdu'l-Bahá's Influence on the History of Black/White Relations in the United States

The early American Bahá'í community was mainly composed of white Americans who were just beginning to understand the tremendous social and historical significance of the Bahá'í teachings on racial unity. It would take them many decades to understand fully and to apply these teachings to their community life. Fortunately for the American Bahá'í community and American race relations, 'Abdu'l-Bahá visited North America in 1912 and both lectured

---

18. 'Abdu'l-Bahá, *Selections* 113.

19. 'Abdu'l-Bahá in Taylor, *Power of Unity* 31.

on and demonstrated the Bahá'í teachings on racial unity and love. His contribution to the betterment of race relations has yet to be properly placed in the annals of American race relations scholarship, but any objective scholar of American race relations studying the period between 1912-1921 would have to take into account the role played by 'Abdu'l-Bahá in the direction of American race relations.

There are several major areas in which 'Abdu'l-Bahá left his mark on American race relations during this period: He infused the Bahá'í teachings on racial unity, love, and fellowship into contemporary discussions on American race relations and thus elevated that discussion to the highest intellectual and spiritual plane in its history. He gave Americans, Bahá'ís and non-Bahá'ís alike, a new spiritual language and racial images with which they could visualize the highest expressions of racial unity. 'Abdu'l-Bahá then modeled the Bahá'í teachings on racial unity, love, and fellowship in such dramatic and loving ways as to leave an indelible imprint on the minds and spirits of those who heard him. Then, after he returned home to what was then Palestine, he encouraged a white American Bahá'í woman to organize a race amity conference that started a Bahá'í tradition still carried on today and is the American Bahá'í community's undisputed contribution to the best tradition of American race relations.

As already mentioned, 'Abdu'l-Bahá had sent a message to the 1911 Universal Race Congress in London in which he explained the importance of the diversity of the human family and compared humankind to a flower garden adorned with different colors and shapes that "enhance the loveliness of each other." The next year, in 1912, 'Abdu'l-Bahá spoke at Howard University, the premier black university in Washington, D.C. According to one of his companions who kept diaries of 'Abdu'l-Bahá's Western tours and lectures, wherever 'Abdu'l-Bahá witnessed racial diversity, he was compelled to call attention to it. During 'Abdu'l-Bahá's talk at Howard University in April of 1912, this companion reported: ". . . here, as elsewhere, when both white and colored people were present, Abdul-Baha seemed happiest."[20]

As he looked over the racially mixed audience at Howard, 'Abdu'l-Bahá remarked: "Today I am most happy, for I see here a gathering of the servants of God. I see white and black sitting together."[21] After two talks the very next day, 'Abdu'l-Bahá was visibly tired as he prepared for the third talk. He was not planning to talk long. But here again, when he saw blacks and whites in the audience, he became inspired.[22] "A meeting such as this seems like a beautiful cluster of precious jewels—pearls, rubies, diamonds, sapphires. It is a source of joy and delight." 'Abdu'l-Bahá then went on to elaborate on the theme of racial

---

20.   Quoted in Ward, 40.

21.   'Abdu'l-Bahá, *Promulgation* 44.

22.   H.M. Balyuzi, *'Abdu'l-Bahá: The Center of the Covenant of Bahá'u'lláh* (London: George Ronald, 1971) 181-82.

unity to an audience that probably had never heard such high praise for a gathering that many white Americans would have frowned upon and just as many black Americans would have avoided. "Whatever is conducive to the unity of the world of mankind is most acceptable and praiseworthy. . . .Therefore, in the world of humanity it is wise and seemly that all the individual members should manifest unity and affinity." Returning once again to his constant use of positive racial images woven into the new language of racial unity and fellowship, he painted a picture for his audience: "In the clustered jewels of the races may the blacks be as sapphires and rubies and the whites as diamonds and pearls. The composite beauty of humanity will be witnessed in their unity and blending."[23] To still another racially mixed audience, 'Abdu'l-Bahá commented: "As I stand here tonight and look upon this assembly, I am reminded curiously of a beautiful bouquet of violets gathered together in varying colors, dark and light."[24]

Realizing the depth of American racism from both his conversations and correspondences with black and white American Bahá'ís years before he visited the United States, 'Abdu'l-Bahá did not miss any opportunity to demonstrate to all Americans, black and white, high and low, young and old, the Bahá'í approach to the racial problems in the United States.[25] While visiting the Bowery Mission area in New York, some poor boys visited 'Abdu'l-Bahá in his room. As the boys filed into the room 'Abdu'l-Bahá greeted each one. The last boy to enter the room was a very dark African-American. Because he was the only black boy in the group he probably felt that 'Abdu'l-Bahá and his host would not accept him. But as an observer reported:

When 'Abdu'l-Bahá saw him His face lighted up with a heavenly smile. He raised His hand with a gesture of princely welcome and exclaimed in a loud voice so that none could fail to hear; that here was a black rose.

The room fell into instant silence. The black face became illumined with a happiness and love hardly of this world. The other boys looked at him with new eyes. I venture to say that he had been called a black—many things, but never before a black rose.[26]

As in the talks to racially mixed audiences, 'Abdu'l-Bahá's repeated comparisons of beautifully diverse flowers and jewels to an equally beautiful mixture of peoples, particularly black and white, transformed the traditional racist color symbolism and imagery into the symbolism and imagery of racial unity. In

---

23. 'Abdu'l-Bahá, *Promulgation* 56-57.

24. 'Abdu'l-Bahá, *Promulgation* 49.

25. For letters from 'Abdu'l-Bahá before his trip to North America, see *Louis G. Gregory, A Heavenly Vista: The Pilgrimage of Louis G. Gregory* (Washington, D.C.: n.p., n.d.).

26. Howard Colby Ives, *Portals to Freedom* (London: George Ronald, 1943) 65.

short, 'Abdu'l-Bahá presented black and white Americans with "new eyes" and a new spiritual language with which to visualize, and therefore to achieve, a spiritual fellowship. By calling upon black and white Americans to see themselves in a new light, as different colored flowers and jewels complementing each other, 'Abdu'l-Bahá enabled them to counter and transcend the racist cultural tendencies so ingrained in the American national character with a flow of radiant imagery and symbolism of racial diversity.

While in the United States 'Abdu'l-Bahá's every act seemed to be calculated to demonstrate the Bahá'í teachings on the supreme importance of love and unity between all members of the human race, especially blacks and whites. Perhaps at no other time and place during his visit to the United States did 'Abdu'l-Bahá demonstrate in so dramatic yet so characteristically gentle and unassuming a way the Bahá'í teachings and principles of racial unity, than at a luncheon held in his honor in Washington, D.C. The luncheon had been arranged by two Bahá'ís, Ali-Kuli Khan, the Persian chargé d'affaires, and Florence Breed Khan, his wife. Some of the guests were members of Washington's social and political elite. Before the luncheon 'Abdu'l-Bahá sent for Louis Gregory, a well-known black Bahá'í. They chatted for a while and when lunch was ready and the guests were seated, 'Abdu'l-Bahá invited Louis Gregory to the luncheon. The assembled guests, including the Bahá'ís, were no doubt surprised not only by 'Abdu'l-Bahá's inviting a black person to an upper-class social affair but even more by the affection and love shown by 'Abdu'l-Bahá for Gregory when he gave the latter the seat of honor on his right. A biographer of Louis Gregory writes of this event: "Gently yet unmistakably 'Abdu'l-Bahá had assaulted the customs of a city that had been scandalized only a decade earlier by President Roosevelt's dinner invitation to Booker T. Washington."[27]

Given the fact that during 'Abdu'l-Bahá's visit to the United States many blacks and whites did not accept interracial marriage, and there were many states that outlawed the practice or did not recognize such unions, 'Abdu'l-Bahá never wavered in his insistence that black Bahá'ís and white Bahá'ís should not only be unified but also should intermarry. Once while he was home in Palestine, he discussed the matter of interracial marriage with several black and white Western Bahá'ís and explored the sexual myths and fears at the core of American racism. His solution was to encourage interracial marriage. Once again as the supreme model of the Bahá'í teachings and principles, he brought together a black American Bahá'í, Louis Gregory, and an English Bahá'í, Louisa Matthew. It was the first black-white interracial marriage between Bahá'ís and became known as the marriage that was encouraged by 'Abdu'l-Bahá himself. This demonstration of Bahá'í teachings and principles proved difficult to accept for some Bahá'ís who doubted that such a union could last in a segregated society, but the marriage lasted for many decades until their deaths

---

27. Morrison, 53.

close to four decades later. Throughout this period the Gregorys became the ultimate American Bahá'í symbol of racial unity, love, and fellowship.[28]

Historians of American race relations in the early twentieth century will one day examine the influence of 'Abdu'l-Bahá's 1912 visit to the United States on certain aspects of American race relations, as well as examine the impact of Bahá'í-initiated race amity conferences on the history of race relations. 'Abdu'l-Bahá had warned American Bahá'ís that bloodshed would take place if America did not solve the racial crisis.

Years later, from his home in Palestine, 'Abdu'l-Bahá initiated a plan to address the racial crisis in America. His plan was to organize "a series of large, well-publicized interracial meetings, conducted not to protest any specific grievance or to seek improvement of the lot of American blacks in some particular way, but to proclaim the oneness of mankind and to promote 'racial amity between black and white Americans'." The first of these conferences took place in 1921 in Washington, D.C., followed by others. Decades later, race amity or unity conferences would become the hallmark of the American Bahá'í community's contribution to American race relations.[29] And this was all due to the manner in which 'Abdu'l-Bahá modeled the Bahá'í teachings on racial unity, love, and fellowship.

Bahá'í Community Practices: The Struggle for Racial Unity, Love, and Fellowship

The American Bahá'í community has been involved in a long struggle to realize the great potential 'Abdu'l-Bahá envisioned for it before, during, and after his visit to the United States. He worked very hard to help the American Bahá'ís realize the connection between racial unity and social progress. He gave them a new spiritual language with which to articulate a new vision of race relations. He demonstrated how a true Bahá'í should approach America's racial problems—even going so far as to encourage the first interracial marriage between a black and a white in the American Bahá'í community.

However, the road to racial unity and harmony has been a long challenging one for the American Bahá'í community. For decades, even while some Bahá'ís labored in the difficult field of race relations, others, particularly whites, struggled with the racial feelings they had inherited from the larger racist society. White- and black-Bahá'ís had both their own separate and joint spiritual battles to fight so as to create a Bahá'í community worthy of the teachings and principles of Bahá'u'lláh and the vision of 'Abdu'l-Bahá. Even after the visit and modeling of racial unity, love, and fellowship by 'Abdu'l-Bahá, some white Bahá'ís in Washington, D.C. still considered racially integrated meetings as "the one serious obstacle to the growth of the cause"[30] in that city. However, in the

28.   Morrison, 63-72, 309-10.

29.   Morrison, 132.

30.   Morrison, 74.

end, motivated by the spiritual teachings, these same white Bahá'ís decided to live up to the high ideals of the Bahá'í teachings on racial unity. The process by which they arrived at this dramatic transformation demonstrated the spiritual power latent in their belief in Bahá'u'lláh's revelation. Morrison says it best in her book *To Move the World*:

> . . .the racial problems in Washington, D.C., from 1914 to 1916 cannot be seen simply as an example of a religious community failing to live up to its ideals. Rather, these early Bahá'ís are revealed as having been immature, deprived of their accustomed leadership, on their own and groping toward the light of understanding. The decision to follow either the Bahá'í way or the way of the world was theirs to make, without even a further word of prompting from 'Abdu'l-Bahá. Thus—however many unresolved feelings may have remained on both sides for many years to come—the 1916 resolution to end the white-only meeting and demonstrably reunite their efforts proved the sincerity of their commitment to a changing order.[31]

White Bahá'ís would have to struggle for decades to overcome the influence of racial segregation on the delicate, still-forming community life of their religion. While the vast majority of American whites had no such challenges to their segregated meetings and felt few moral qualms about their segregated meetings—many believing that segregation was sanctioned by God and the Bible,[32]—white Bahá'ís had clear and explicit teachings in the Bahá'í holy writings and teachings, as well as equally clear and explicit instructions and guidelines from Shoghi Effendi, that racial segregation was morally wrong and a direct violation of the Bahá'í teachings. Furthermore, white Bahá'ís were instructed to live up to the Bahá'í teachings on racial unity, love, and fellowship. Only the most spiritually courageous white Americans with a deep belief in the world-embracing principles of Bahá'u'lláh were willing to make such a commitment.

Blacks had been involved in the American Bahá'í community since the 1890s[33] and had to suffer through what Morrison referred to as the white Bahá'ís' "groping toward the light of understanding." Often, this meant that black Bahá'ís had to carry the burden of transcending the racism of the white Bahá'ís in order to live up to their role and tasks of creating racial unity within the larger society. This was very difficult because black Bahá'ís, seeing the Bahá'í Faith through the eyes of an oppressed racial minority, expected white Bahá'ís to transcend their racism. When white Bahá'ís failed to live up to the

---

31.   Morrison, 81.

32.   Everett Tilson, *Segregation and the Bible* (Nashville: Abingdon Press, n.d.) 15–28.

33.   See Gwen Etter-Lewis, unpublished paper on black Bahá'í women.

Bahá'í teachings on racial unity, black Bahá'ís felt betrayed. For example, in 1937, when one of the two most prominent black Bahá'ís in Chicago, Ellsworth Blackwell, was "barred from serving as a guide at the [Bahá'í] Temple because of his race," he wrote a letter to Shoghi Effendi in which he said in part:

> From my knowledge of the [Bahá'í] teachings it appears to me that the Principles of Bahá'u'lláh are being violated within His Temple by the Believers. The only apparent excuse for their policy is that the presence of Colored guides would offend people of the White race. As you no doubt realize the aforementioned large touring groups are composed of all nationalities and races. Are we supposed to alter the Principles to accommodate the prejudices of the people outside the Cause, particularly within our own institutions? And, may I ask, when are we to begin to live the Teachings of Bahá'u'lláh?[34]

Fortunately for all concerned, the appropriate Bahá'í local and national institutions responded very well to what had been the residual effect of a past policy of racial segregation. The earlier policy of barring black Bahá'ís from serving as guides was eliminated as a result of consultation on the issue in the light of 'Abdu'l-Bahá's repeated warnings about the American racial crisis.

Shoghi Effendi recognized the humiliation, pain, and anguish black Bahá'ís were experiencing as the result of white Bahá'ís' racial attitudes. In a letter to a black Bahá'í woman, sent on his behalf, he said that he was "well aware that the conditions within the ranks of the believers in respect to race prejudice is [*sic*] far from being as it should be. However he feels very strongly that it presents a challenge to both white and coloured believers." Shoghi Effendi, then gave the following advice to his black fellow Bahá'ís: ". . .it is incumbent upon the [N]egro believers to rise above this great test which the attitude of some of their white brethren may present. They must prove their innate equality not by words but by deeds. They must," Shoghi Effendi stressed, "accept the *Cause* of Bahá'u'lláh for the sake of the Cause, love it, and cling to it, and teach it, and fight for it as *their* own Cause, forgetful of the shortcomings of others. Any other attitude is unworthy of their faith"(italics in original). He then reminded the black believers how Bahá'u'lláh had praised blacks: "Proud and happy in the praises which even Bahá'u'lláh Himself had bestowed upon them, they must feel He revealed Himself for them and every other downtrodden race, loves them, and will help them to attain their destiny." Pointing to the fact that "the whole race question in America is a national one and of great importance." Shoghi Effendi expressed the concern that ". . .the [N]egro friends must not waste their precious opportunity to serve the Faith, in these momentous days, by dwelling on the admitted short comings of the white friends. They must arise and serve and teach, confident of the future they are building, a future in which we know these barriers will have once and for all been overcome. [35]

---

34. Mark Lloyd Perry, "The Chicago Bahá'í Community, 1921-1939." Unpublished dissertation, University of Chicago, 1986, 299-300; also in *World Order* (Winter 1985-86): 41-60.

35. Morrison, 296.

Shoghi Effendi's letter to black Bahá'ís emphasized the role black Bahá'ís had to play in the spiritual unification of America. As he explained to another believer: "The more Negroes who become Bahá'ís, the greater the leaven will be within their own race, working for harmony and friendship between these two bodies of American citizens: the white and the colored."[36] In addition to the role they could play "as leaven. . .within their own race, working for harmony and friendship between. . . .white and black," Shoghi Effendi pointed to still another contribution blacks could make: "The qualities of heart so richly possessed by the Negro are much needed in the world today—their great capacity for faith, their loyalty and devotion to their religion when once they believe, their purity of heart. God has richly endowed them, and their contribution to the Cause is much needed. . . ."[37]

For all these reasons, Bahá'ís in the United States had to help each other to build a model community reflecting racial unity, love, and fellowship. As the years passed, they have struggled with this "the most challenging issue." They have not always been able to avoid all the "pitfalls" along the "long and thorny road," but they have continued to try. In 1986, the National Race Unity Committee of the Bahá'ís of the United States took the Bahá'í community another step along this path with the following insightful and challenging words:

> Our American Bahá'í community may soon possess a majority of members who are from minority populations in the United States. Inevitably, our culture as a Bahá'í community must also change. Such a change will manifest itself initially through an increasing appreciation for the cultural offerings—music, food, festivities, manners of speech and dress—of blacks, Hispanics, Native Americans, Persians, Southeast Asians, and others in the Bahá'í community. But ultimately we must become multicultural so that our community life acquires a character that is flexible, versatile, creative, and blessed with a wide repertoire of cultural responses to daily Bahá'í life. These patterns of our collective life also deserve our attention because they serve to become magnets for the spiritual energy that quickens our community life. As 'Abdu'l-Bahá guides us: "It is impossible to unite unless united.". . .

> The National Race Unity Committee is eager for the friends to meditate on the question of unity, to develop a longing to see it manifest in all its beauty in their lives and in their communities. . . .[38]

In the final pages of *The Promise of World Peace*, a statement on peace from the Universal House of Justice, the supreme governing body of the Bahá'í

---

36. On behalf of Shoghi Effendi, letter dated 12/18/43 to an individual believer, quoted in *The Power of Unity*, 107.

37. Helen Hornsby, ed., *Lights of Guidance*, 2d ed. (New Delhi, India: Bahá'í Publishing Trust, 1988) 532.

38. *The Power of Unity* x-xi.

Faith, addressed "To the Peoples of the World," the following statement: "If the Bahá'í experience can contribute in whatever measure to reinforcing hope in the unity of the human race, we are happy to offer it as a model for study."[39] Perhaps the same should be said of the American Bahá'í experience in their long struggle to create racial unity, love, and fellowship among their fellow Americans.

The Most Challenging Issue: Spiritual Guidelines for Achieving Racial Unity, Love, and Fellowship within the American Bahá'í Community

One of the most far-reaching statements on American race relations as related to the Bahá'í community was published in 1938 in a book entitled *The Advent of Divine Justice*.[40] The section on race relations, called, "The Most Challenging Issue," constitutes one of the most insightful statements on American racial problems in the history of American race relations literature. Written by Shoghi Effendi, who for decades had been guiding the American Bahá'í community down the "long and thorny path" of racial conflicts, "The Most Challenging Issue" has become the most well-known and often-quoted formulation of the roles of black Bahá'ís and white Bahá'ís in the resolution of racial problems both within and outside of the American Bahá'í community.

"As to racial prejudice, the corrosion of which, for well nigh a century, has bitten into the fiber, and attacked the whole social structure of American society, it should be regarded as constituting the most vital and challenging issue confronting the Bahá'í community at the present stage of its evolution." Such a challenging statement by the spiritual head of the Bahá'í Faith on an issue upon which no major secular or religious American leader had ever taken so bold a stand at once made clear to every Bahá'í the "vital and challenging" nature of the racial problem. This would not be an easy problem to solve. Shoghi Effendi knew only too well that Bahá'ís would have to prepare themselves for a grave challenge. "The ceaseless exertions which this issue of paramount importance calls for, the sacrifices it must impose, the care and vigilance it demands, the moral courage and fortitude it requires, the tact and sympathy it necessitates," Shoghi Effendi explained, "invest this problem, which the American believers are still far from having satisfactorily resolved, with an urgency and importance that cannot be overestimated." Every member of the American Bahá'í community was called upon to work on the problem. "White and Negro,

39.   The Universal House of Justice, The *Promise of World Peace* (Haifa: Bahá'í World Centre, 1985) 12.

40.   Shoghi Effendi, *The Advent of Divine Justice*, 4th ed. (Wilmette: Bahá'í Publishing Trust, 1984).

high and low, young and old, whether newly converted to the Faith or not, all who stand identified with it must participate in, and lend their assistance, each according to his or her capacity, experience, and opportunities, to the common task of fulfilling the instructions, realizing the hopes, and following the example of 'Abdu'l-Bahá."[41] 'Abdu'l-Bahá embodied the spiritual qualities Bahá'ís were instructed to emulate if they desired to be good Bahá'ís. By emulating 'Abdu'l-Bahá, both black Bahá'ís and white Bahá'ís would be more spiritually attuned to racial unity, love, and fellowship. As explained by Shoghi Effendi, neither black Bahá'ís nor white Bahá'ís for whatever reason could place the burden of resolving the racial problem on the other group. "Whether colored or noncolored, neither race has the right, or can conscientiously claim, to be regarded as absolved from such an obligation, as having realized such hopes, or having faithfully followed such an example." Bahá'ís, Shoghi Effendi warned, still had a long road to travel. "A long and thorny road, beset with pitfalls, still remains untraveled, both by the white and the Negro exponents of the redeeming Faith of Bahá'u'lláh. On the distance they cover, and the manner in which they travel that road," Shoghi Effendi cautioned, "must depend, to an extent which few among them can imagine, the operation of those intangible influences which are indispensable to the spiritual triumph of the American believers and the material success of their newly launched enterprise."[42]

Shoghi Effendi called upon the American Bahá'í community to "call to mind, fearlessly and determinedly, the example and conduct of 'Abdu'l-Bahá while in their midst. Let them remember His courage, His genuine love, His informal and indiscriminating fellowship, His contempt for and impatience of criticism, tempered by His tact and wisdom." They were to "revive and perpetuate the memory of those unforgettable and historic episodes and occasions on which He so strikingly demonstrated His keen sense of justice, His spontaneous sympathy for the downtrodden, His ever-abiding sense of the oneness of the human race, His overflowing love for its members. . . ." Any discrimination "against any race, on the ground of its being socially backward, politically immature, and numerically in a minority, is a flagrant violation of the spirit that animates the Faith of Bahá'u'lláh. The consciousness of any division or cleavage in its ranks is alien to its very purpose, principles, and ideals."[43]

Once Bahá'ís have "fully recognized the claim of its [the Bahá'í Faith's] Author, and, by identifying themselves with its Administrative Order, accepted unreservedly the principles and laws embodied in its teachings," Shoghi Effendi explained, "every differentiation of class, creed, or colour must automatically be obliterated, and never be allowed, under any pretext, and however great the pressure of events or of public opinion, to reassert itself."[44]

---

41. Shoghi Effendi, 33-34.

42. Shoghi Effendi, 34.

43   Shoghi Effendi, 34-35.

44. Shoghi Effendi, 35.

The very act of becoming a Bahá'í commits one to live by the Bahá'í teachings on racial unity. There is no way around this. The Bahá'í teachings were clear; no bias of any sort was allowed, no matter how "great the pressure of events or public opinion." This was written in 1938 when segregation in the schools and racially restrictive covenants were sanctioned by the United States Constitution and the Federal Housing Administration unabashedly supported segregated housing. Baseball, the most popular sport in America, had not yet been desegregated, and the Armed Services of the United States, soon to go into the Second World War, still boasted a racially segregated system. How were the American Bahá'ís expected to resist such an array of the most powerful forces and institutions in the United States that were solidly behind the racial status quo? Shoghi Effendi not only expected them to stand firm on the Bahá'í teachings and principles related to racial unity and fellowship but also in certain situations as a means to achieve certain goals to discriminate in favor of minorities within the Bahá'í communities.

If any discrimination is at all to be tolerated, it should be a discrimination not against, but rather in favor of the minority, be it racial or otherwise. Unlike the nations and peoples of the earth, be they of the East or of the West, democratic or authoritarian, communist or capitalist, whether belonging to the Old World or the New, who either ignore, trample upon, or extirpate, the racial, religious, or political minorities within the sphere of their jurisdiction, every organized community enlisted under the banner of Bahá'u'lláh should feel it to be its first and inescapable obligation to nurture, encourage, and safeguard every minority belonging to any faith, race, class, or nation within it. So great and vital is this principle that in such circumstances, as when an equal number of ballots have been cast in an election, or where the qualifications for any office are balanced as between the various races, faiths or nationalities within the community, priority should unhesitatingly be accorded the party representing the minority, and this for no other reason except to stimulate and encourage it, and afford it an opportunity to further the interests of the community.[45]

Shoghi Effendi's application of Bahá'í teachings and principles to minority issues within the Bahá'í community represented a profound and unprecedented model of how communities should treat their minorities so as to enable them better to serve and contribute to the larger social order. One can only imagine the tremendous social and economic progress the United States could have made if local and national leaders had applied Shoghi Effendi's suggestions to the racial problems. Had white America seen as "its first and inescapable obligation to nurture, encourage, and safeguard" Native peoples and blacks as well as other racial minorities, the country would have been light years ahead in material and spiritual progress. The policy of discriminating in favor of the minority so as to "stimulate and encourage it, and afford it an opportunity to further the

45. Shoghi Effendi, 35.

interest of the community" could have only been conceived by one who believes in the organic unity of the human race. Outside of such a context of spiritual unity, the policy would be interpreted as a form of "reverse discrimination." Tainted by the pervasive influence of racism and unable or unwilling to think of racial minorities as members of "their [white] communities," many white Americans would fail to see how such a application of positive discrimination on behalf of racial minorities could benefit them and the larger community as well. That Shoghi Effendi understood and shared this application of Bahá'í teachings to the racial problems in the American Bahá'í community is testimony to the profound relevance of these teachings to American race relations. But there was much more in "The Most Challenging Issue."

Continuing "in the light of this principle," Shoghi Effendi explained how the Bahá'í community should go out of its way to arrange its affairs to encourage minorities to participate in all areas of its community life:

> In the light of this principle, and bearing in mind the extreme desirability of having the minority elements participate and share responsibility in the conduct of Bahá'í activity, it should be the duty of every Bahá'í community so to arrange its affairs that in cases where individuals belonging to the divers minority elements within it are already qualified and fulfill the necessary requirements, Bahá'í representative institutions, . . . may have represented on them as many of these divers elements, racial or otherwise, as possible. The adoption of such a course, and faithful adherence to it, would not only be a source of inspiration and encouragement to those elements that are numerically small and inadequately represented, but would demonstrate to the world at large the universality and representative character of the Faith of Bahá'u'lláh, and the freedom of His followers from the taint of those prejudices which have already wrought such havoc in the domestic affairs, as well as the foreign relationships, of the nations.[46]

Shoghi Effendi understood the pervasive nature of American racism and how it could poison Bahá'í community life, particularly at a time when European and American racism was rampant. The American Bahá'í community was instructed by Shoghi Effendi to adopt the watchword "freedom from racial prejudice" to aid them in their struggles against racism. A watchword can be a motto, a cry, or a slogan, but it usually means something that embodies a principle.

> Freedom from racial prejudice, in any of its forms, should, at such a time as this when an increasingly large section of the human race is falling a victim to its devastating ferocity, be adopted as the watchword of the entire body of the American believers, in whichever state they reside, in whatever circles they move, whatever their age, traditions, tastes, and habits. It should be consistently demonstrated in every phase of their activity and life,

---

46. Shoghi Effendi, 35-36.

whether in the Bahá'í community or outside it, in public or in private, formally as well as informally, individually as well as in their official capacity as organized groups, committees and Assemblies.[47]

Here again, Shoghi Effendi clearly set the guidelines for combatting racism and promoting the Bahá'í principle and model of racial unity. Living in a state that practiced racism did not excuse Bahá'ís from working on their racial attitudes and behavior. If they belonged to social circles that segregated against blacks or other racial minorities, they were obviously violating the principles of the Bahá'í Faith. Whatever their "age, traditions, tastes, and habits," they were obligated to work on freeing themselves from racial prejudices. Furthermore, Shoghi Effendi told them to demonstrate freedom from racial prejudice consistently in every phase of their lives, both inside and outside the Bahá'í community. Being free from racial prejudice only within the Bahá'í community was far from sufficient. The Bahá'í teachings, as explained by Shoghi Effendi and applied by him to the American racial problems, demanded much more from Bahá'ís, especially whites, who had much racist cultural baggage that had to be eliminated.

What more could the American Bahá'ís do to rid themselves of racial prejudice after demonstrating the Bahá'í teachings in their public and private lives? They should, Shoghi Effendi wrote, "deliberately" cultivate freedom from racial prejudice "through the various and everyday opportunities, no matter how insignificant, that present themselves, whether in their homes, their business offices, their schools and colleges, their social parties and recreation grounds, their Bahá'í meetings, conferences, conventions, summer schools and Assemblies."[48] Addressing their national governing body, Shoghi Effendi told American Bahá'ís that, freedom from racial prejudice "should, above all else, become the keynote of the policy of that august body which, in its capacity as the national representative, and the director and coordinator of the affairs of the community, must set the example, and facilitate the application of such a vital principle to the lives and activities of those whose interests it safeguards and represents."[49]

After explaining why and how the American Bahá'í community should work on freeing itself from racial prejudice, Shoghi Effendi pointed out that Bahá'u'lláh said

that the various races of humankind lend a composite harmony and beauty of color to the whole. Let all associate, therefore, in this great human garden even as flowers grow and blend together side by side without discord or disagreement between them.[50]

---

47. Shoghi Effendi, 36.

48. Shoghi Effendi, 36.

49. Shoghi Effendi, 36-37.

50. Bahá'u'lláh quoted in Shoghi Effendi, 37.

Bahá'u'lláh also "once compared the colored people to the black pupil of the eye surrounded by the white. In this black pupil is seen the reflection of that which is before it, and through it the light of the spirit shineth forth."[51] Of all Bahá'u'lláh's statements on racial unity, this is probably the one most favored by black American Bahá'ís because of the very positive symbolism given to blackness. In a culture where whiteness has always been the unquestioned symbol of spiritual purity and blackness the symbol of the lack of spiritual purity, Bahá'u'lláh's teachings on race transformed the negative meaning of black/white symbolism infused in Western culture by centuries of ethnocentrism and racism into a black/white symbol of spiritual unity. This meaning was not lost upon American Bahá'ís. Those who reflected upon it could not help but be transformed: blacks could see themselves in a new spiritual light as the "black pupil" reflecting "that which is before it," and through which "the light of the spirit shineth forth." They could in fact rejoice in this affirmation of their spirituality embodied in such a powerful color symbolism by the founder of the Faith Himself. White Bahá'ís could free themselves of all the negative cultural connotations Western religious thought had attributed to the symbolism of blackness. Both black Bahá'ís and white Bahá'ís could also rejoice in the fact that for the first time in Western religious thought there was now a color symbolism that did not cast black and white as spiritual opposites but as spiritual complements to each other.

To assist Bahá'ís in carrying out their dual roles of applying Bahá'í principles to the solution of the problems of racism and racial conflicts, both within their community and in the larger society, Shoghi Effendi provided the following instructions and guidelines. First he reminded them that "tremendous effort is required by both races if their outlook, their manners, and conduct are to reflect, in this darkened age, the spirit and teachings of the Faith of Bahá'u'lláh. Casting away once and for all the fallacious doctrine of racial superiority," he said, "with all its attendant evils, confusion, and miseries, and welcoming and encouraging the intermixture of races, and tearing down the barriers that now divide them, they should each endeavor, day and night, to fulfill their particular responsibilities in the common task which so urgently faces them." While working jointly on this "common task," he reminded them to remember 'Abdu'l-Bahá's warnings about racial conflicts in America. "Let them, while each is attempting to contribute its share to the solution of this perplexing problem," Shoghi Effendi wrote, "call to mind the warnings of 'Abdu'l-Bahá, and visualize, while there is yet time, the dire consequences that must follow if this challenging and unhappy situation that faces the entire American nation is not definitely remedied."[52] He then outlined guidelines for Bahá'ís to work on in

---

51.   'Abdu'l-Bahá quoted in Shoghi Effendi, 37.

52.   Shoghi Effendi, 40.

their joint efforts to remedy the racial problems facing their country. Addressing his white fellow Bahá'ís, Shoghi Effendi wrote:

Let the white make a supreme effort in their resolve to contribute their share to the solution of this problem, to abandon once for all their usually inherent and at times subconscious sense of superiority, to correct their tendency towards revealing a patronizing attitude towards the members of the other race, to persuade them through their intimate, spontaneous and informal association with them of the genuineness of their friendship and the sincerity of their intentions, and to master their impatience of any lack of responsiveness on the part of a people who have received, for so long a period, such grievous and slow-healing wounds.[53]

Turning next to his black fellow Bahá'ís, Shoghi Effendi said:

Let the Negroes, through a corresponding effort on their part, show by every means in their power the warmth of their response, their readiness to forget the past, and their ability to wipe out every trace of suspicion that may still linger in their hearts and minds.[54]

Having given both black Bahá'ís and white Bahá'ís separate but complementary guidelines for their joint task, Shoghi Effendi then addressed them as members of a spiritual community upon which the ultimate resolution of American racial problems depended:

Let neither think that the solution of so vast a problem is a matter that exclusively concerns the other. Let neither think that such a problem can either easily or immediately be resolved. Let neither think that they can wait confidently for the solution of this problem until the initiative has been taken, and the favorable circumstances created, by agencies that stand outside the orbit of their Faith. Let neither think that anything short of genuine love, extreme patience, true humility, consummate tact, sound initiative, mature wisdom, and deliberate, persistent, and prayerful effort, can succeed in blotting out the stain which this patent evil has left on the fair name of their common country. Let them rather believe, and be firmly convinced, that on their mutual understanding, their amity, and sustained cooperation, must depend, more than on any other force or organization operating outside the circle of their Faith, the deflection of that dangerous course so greatly feared by 'Abdu'l-Bahá, and the materialization of the hopes He cherished for their joint contribution to the fulfillment of that country's glorious destiny.[55]

---

53.   Shoghi Effendi, 40.

54.   Shoghi Effendi, 40.

55.   Shoghi Effendi, 40-41

EPILOGUE

CHAPTER 8

A TRANSFORMATIONAL AGENDA
FOR RACIAL UNITY AND SOCIAL PROGRESS

> As I stand here and look upon thousands of Negro faces, and the thousands of white faces, intermingled like the waters of a river, I see only one face—the face of the future.
>
> Dr. Martin Luther King, Jr.

Developing an Agenda that Truly Transforms People and Communities

This book has examined aspects of the history of race relations in the United States. We now have some understanding of how the tradition of white racism evolved and poisoned the very core of American society. We also have some understanding of another tradition in American history: the tradition of interracial struggle for racial justice, unity, love, and fellowship. This latter great tradition has expanded the vision of America, from one that saw this country as a land given by God to whites as their racial manifest destiny to one in which all of humankind could develop a model multiracial community that would be "the city on the hill" for all humankind to emulate. The historic tension between these two opposing traditions has been at the heart of racial problems in the United States. These tensions are still playing themselves out in a million different settings in peoples' hearts, minds, and souls in families and communities throughout the United States and every other multiracial society in the world. The struggle for racial justice, unity, fellowship, and love is at heart a struggle that transcends black/white relations. Rather, it is a struggle driven by the oldest vision and tradition of human history: the struggle to recognize our common humanity, our organic oneness. No matter what form this struggle has assumed—political, economic, cultural—its deepest roots are spiritual in nature. When individuals and communities are connected with the spiritual roots of these struggles, they are transformed. They become new people. When they are disconnected from the spiritual roots of their struggle, they gain power, but they are not transformed. They are merely new faces in the same human drama. The script does not change. They are not elevated as human beings and communities. The process for human betterment either stagnates or regresses. Therefore, all struggles for any form of justice must (if their objective is to transform people and communities in a way that will elevate them and the larger world) be grounded in spiritual principles. The present struggle for racial justice, unity, fellowship, and love is in need of an agenda that can guide it along the path to its fullest potential—that of a spiritual leaven for multiracial/multicultural communities around the world.

A transformative agenda is one that in the process of seeking racial justice, unity, fellowship, and love transforms and elevates peoples and communities. A transformative agenda explains the interconnection between all the above elements and social progress. A transformative agenda for racial unity and social progress seeks a basic change in perceptions and values about human beings. It seeks to inculcate in all people an appreciation of the organic oneness of the human family. It unabashedly embraces and advocates love for one's fellow human beings as a prerequisite for building and healing communities.

Changing Our Perceptions and Values About People and Communities

New perceptions and values about relationships among peoples and communities are essential to any transformative agenda for racial unity and social progress. Unity must be understood as the key precondition for all forms of social progress. What we need is a new paradigm to help us see old problems in new ways. Psychiatrist H. B. Danesh, discusses one such "new way" in his ground-breaking book *Unity: The Creative Foundation of Peace*: "The unity paradigm is an all-encompassing concept, at the same time simple and complex, individual and universal, concrete and abstract, emotional and intellectual, material and spiritual." This unity paradigm, Danesh explains, "challenges us to look at ourselves in new ways and to reappraise our previously-held conceptions in the light of this new perspective on human reality."[1] In the light of centuries of disunity among all kinds of peoples, such a paradigm strains credulity. One has only to survey the present world to see compelling evidence to the contrary. Yet Danesh's argument is persuasive:

The story of mankind's disunity is also that of its unity. In its march toward maturity, humanity has achieved many remarkable acts of unity, such as the successive creation of family, clan, tribe, state, and nation. Humanity has also achieved a greater degree of understanding and empathy among various races and ethnic groups, and we have seen the powerful contemporary movement for achieving equality between men and women, the remarkable increase in world consciousness concerning the need for a new world order, and, finally the creation of multinational organizations and world agencies as first steps towards the achievement of unity.[2]

Although Danesh recognizes that these "accomplishments have contributed to the collective growth of humanity, helping mankind to arrive at its present stage of development. However," he cautions, "these are limited unities, no

---

1. Hossain B. Danesh, *Unity: The Creative Foundation of Peace* (Ottawa: Bahá'í Studies Publications, 1986) 85.

2. Danesh, 86-87.

longer appropriate for the needs of humanity today. The emergence of a global society and a united world demand wider unity, the absence of which has made all other types of unity inoperative and even dangerous."[3]

To make his point concerning the limited power of lesser unities, Danesh quotes 'Abdu'l-Bahá, who said:

> From these limited unities mentioned only limited outcomes proceed whereas unlimited unity produces unlimited result. For instance, from the limited unity of race or nationality the results at most are limited. It is like a family living alone and solitary; there are no unlimited or universal outcomes from it.
>
> The unity which is productive of unlimited results is first a unity of mankind. . . .[4]

This focus on unity is a vital aspect of the transformational agenda for racial unity and social progress. Anyone surveying the contemporary racial scene in the United States knows that whites and blacks are still the most racially segregated and polarized races in American society. Most suburban whites and central city blacks not only live in vastly different physical worlds but also hold drastically different views of each other, developed over the decades and transmitted through racial folklore. Since the end of the Civil Rights Movement, major segments of these two communities have fought pitched ideological, political, and even physical battles on a hundred scattered battlefields, from inner-city schools to college campuses, from factories to boardrooms.

Ironically, while blacks and whites are divided on many issues, they are at the same time united on many others. While many blacks and Jews fight over affirmative action, they both celebrate the birthday of Martin Luther King, Jr. Many young and old, black Americans and white Americans love the same music and even copy each others' cultural styles. Black street kids' "rappin'" has penetrated to the heart of most, if not all, white suburbs. Movie-goers of both races crowd in line to see black comics such as Richard Pryor and Eddie Murphy. Many blacks and whites work side-by-side everyday, year in, year out. They lunch together, jog together, share stories of their families, some even visit each others' homes, and a few marry and raise families. This list could go on, but the point is clear: notwithstanding the many problems and conflicts that still exist between blacks and whites, there are many points of unity and cooperation which can collectively contribute to a transformational agenda for racial unity and social progress.

Here is where the unity paradigm is most appropriate to contemporary race relations, not only in the United States but also in other multiracial societies. All racial groups have to be educated to understand that at this stage of human evolution on this planet, where interdependence is a structural and inter-group

---

3. Danesh, 87.

4. Quoted in Danesh, 87; *Bahá'í World Faith* 257.

reality, *everyone*, no matter who they are or where they are on the social scale, has a vital role to play in solving the problems associated with racism. This calls for nothing less than a unity of vision and purpose. A transformational agenda based upon the unity paradigm proceeds from the assumption that we are all members of one organic family and community. Whatever hurts one of us hurts us all and retards the full development of our common good. Conversely, whatever profits the least of us profits us all. Such an agenda would help those white males who see affirmative action policies and programs solely in terms of how they benefit racial minorities and women to see them instead as enabling minorities and women to contribute more to the common good from which they as white males would also obviously benefit. Applying the unity paradigm to the problems of the cities would enable black central cities and white suburbs to transform their antagonisms into creative strategies to develop the human resources of the *entire* region. All it takes is the realization that in an increasingly interdependent metro-area, state, nation, and world unity is the only path to individual and collective growth and development. Only one barrier stands in the way of achieving the unity that could make the above possible: the lack of vision to see that social progress in every multiracial society in the world is inexorably linked to racial unity. The first building block of the transformational agenda is to impart this vision to those who are commited to racial justice, unity, and social progress.

The Building Blocks of a Transformational Agenda for Racial and Social Progress

The Vision: The Organic Unity of the Human Race

To create a truly racially unified society in which all member races are bonded together by genuine ties of love, respect, and fellowship, there must be a powerful and inspiring vision of what we want to become as a community. We must see ourselves as the rose garden 'Abdu'l-Bahá spoke of, blending together in beauty and harmony. We must be able to visualize loving and caring for each other as members of one family. We must come to feel and sense the power we will have as the result of combining our respective racial talents, skills, perspectives, and insights. This vision must be so all-compelling as to enable all member races to relate to each other as one race—the human race. Once this vision is firmly implanted in the hearts and minds of a critical mass of sincere people from various racial backgrounds, we will become the leaven for the spiritual and social transformation of the entire society. We must impart this vision to our children and youth. Our children should be taught to look for signs of our common humanity. Teachers should inculcate not only recognition of the great heritages of various cultural and racial groups but also the more important recognition and celebration of the organic unity of our species.[5] Then discussions of the history and culture of various groups will not disintegrate into excessive pride, ethnocentrism, envy, competition, or feelings of inferiority. Once children understand that they are linked to every other human being, they will began to feel a kinship with all peoples.

Building on the Tradition of People Working Together

After fixing upon the vision to guide us along the path toward racial unity, we must then begin building upon the already existing tradition of people working together. In short, we do not have to re-invent the proverbial wheel. There are many interracial organizations and groups working for the realization of a racially just, cooperative, and caring society. From Focus Hope in Detroit to the Council on Interracial Books for Children in New York to the Interracial Family Alliance in Houston, a growing number of interracial organizations and groups are working to build a racially just and caring society.[6]

Interracial Friendships

A transformational agenda for racial unity and social progress must include the vast reservoir of interracial friendships that often goes untapped. Many of these friendships have already evolved into highly developed forms of human bonding, capable of generating the healing influences so urgently needed in fragmented and wounded sectors of our multiracial community. The most highly evolved of these interracial friendships can offer us models of how best to heal interracial conflicts such as the present conflicts between some Jews and blacks as well as some blacks and Koreans in certain urban communities. Interracial friendships are the oldest forms of the positive tradition of race relations in the history of American race relations. In the 1970s, a white woman and a black woman discussed their interracial friendship in a book entitled *Interracial Bonds*. The white friend commented:

> There are many divisive forces in our society that mitigate against the chances of interracial friendships developing beyond the superficial level. It even amazes me today as I write this and meditate upon the forces in my background which were set in motion in order to prevent such a friendship from ever forming, that I feel compelled to acknowledge the fact that Adah Askew is one of my closest and most intimate friends, one whom I love very dearly.[7]

---

5. For a good description of the form such education to eliminate such prejudice might take, see Susan Clay Stoddart "Education and Moral Development in Children" *The Journal for Bahá'í Studies,* vol.1, no.1, 1989 (Ottawa: Association for Bahá'í Studies).

6. See the annual interracial march by Focus/Hope in the *Detroit Free Press,* October 15, 1990; "The Council on Interracial Books for Children," leaflet; For information on interracial families, see *Communique,* the official newsletter of the Interracial Family Alliance.

7. Gloria Feman Orenstein, "A Friendship: Part One," in Rhonda Goldstein Blumberg and Wendell James Royce, *Interracial Bonds* (New York: General Hall, 1979) 175.

Her black friend wrote these words about her:

I've lived next door to Gloria for the past nine years and as time has passed our friendship has grown. The intensity of our relationship amazes many people. Perhaps its because I'm black and Gloria is white that our closeness surprises folks. . . .The ties which bind Gloria and me are deep. They have withstood the "causes célèbres" of us both—the emergence of my black awareness and Gloria's feminism.[8]

There are thousands of such genuine interracial friendships that we ignore or see as too marginal to make a difference. Too many of us view these relationships as just isolated interpersonal interracial adventures that rarely last beyond the special circumstances that produce them. While some interracial friendships are of such a nature, enough are genuine and strong enough to tap for a transformational agenda. We must remember that much of the transformation from racism and racial conflicts has occurred within the bonds of interracial friendships. This is the best-kept secret in contemporary American race relations.

Healing Old Wounds and Creating Unity in Fragmented Communities: Blacks and Jews, and Koreans and Blacks

Any transformational agenda for racial unity and social progress must work on healing the wounds of many blacks and Jews who in the heat of their separate struggles to address their needs have strained their traditional relationship. In some cases, they have both afflicted each other so severely with their accusations and counter-accusations that the possibility of reconciliation now seems remote if not highly improbable. Yet, many blacks and Jews are still working together in areas where they do not have to compromise their particular agendas. This unity in diversity is a reality of pragmatic racial/ethnic politics in any pluralistic society. However, a transformational agenda demands much more from both of these long-time allies. Since blacks and Jews have had one of the longest and most effective working relationships of any racial/ethnic groups in recent American history, their combined cultural and spiritual influence is urgently needed to achieve racial unity and social progress. However much some African-Americans and Jews might want to put all their joint history in struggling for social and economic justice behind them and concentrate on their own agendas, the fact is that those very agendas are inextricably linked to developments within the larger society which the transformational agenda must address. Racial justice, unity, love, and fellowship cannot be achieved without the synergistic force of black/Jewish unity and cooperation. Notwithstanding the conflicts between these two traditional allies, they have

---

8. Adah Askew, "A Friendship: Part Two," in Blumberg and Roye, 186-89.

developed the highest form of interracial friendship and inter-group cooperation, love, and fellowship in the history of black/white relations in this country.
This fact alone demands that we work to heal the rifts between these two long-
time friends so that they can contribute their great spiritual powers to the
transformation of American race relations.

The recent conflicts between Korean-American merchants and African-
American customers in New York and other cities reflect another form of fragmentation within the increasingly diverse American society. It is an old problem
with some new faces. It also involves conflicts of racial/ethnic group agendas
and can only be partially solved through traditional means. Both Korean-
Americans and African-Americans need to see their problems from the perspective of the unity paradigm that can more effectively address both groups'
problems. Here again, as with blacks and Jews, Koreans and blacks will need
the assistance of those who have the vision of a truly unified multiracial society
as well as the skills and determination to carry out the transformational agenda
for racial unity and social progress.

A Footnote on South Africa

A truly racially unified American can offer invaluable assistance to South
Africa as that country moves to the post-apartheid stage of race relations. We
could humbly offer our mistakes and successes in particular areas of race
relations and perhaps save them the social costs of repeating those mistakes. If
we are true to our greatest potential as a multiracial society (many South
Africans prefer the term "non-racial"), we might even be able to work with
them in transforming their society into one of the greatest example of non-racial
unity in the modern world.

Biographical Note

Richard W. Thomas is an associate professor in history and urban affairs at Michigan State University. In 1974, he helped design the Department of Racial and Ethnic Studies at the university where he designed and taught courses until the demise of the department in 1980. He has taught courses in African-American history and race relations at various universities for over twenty years. In 1986, he was one of two American scholars invited by the Centre for Research in Ethnic Relations at the University of Warwick, at Coventry, England, to discuss the racial conflicts in urban communities in the United States and England. He is also founder and president of New World Associates, Inc., a consulting firm in the area of race relations and diversity issues. Thomas has published articles and chapters in the fields of race relations and African-American history. He is a co-author of *Detroit: Race and Uneven Development.* His forthcoming book *Black Detroit* is to be published by Indiana University Press.